A.M.Klein

Canada – *pp* viii–ix (Ross), x

K's weakness xiii, xv
62–5 "polemics"
63
(65) re humour in Can. lit
(conn. puritanism)
NB — consider this

re Ben Shahn, calligraphy etc
p 55

VOLUMES READY IN THE RYERSON SERIES

Critical Views on Canadian Writers
MICHAEL GNAROWSKI, Series Editor

CRITICAL VIEWS ON CANADIAN WRITERS

A.M. Klein

Edited and with an Introduction by
TOM MARSHALL

MICHAEL GNAROWSKI, Series Editor

THE RYERSON PRESS
TORONTO WINNIPEG VANCOUVER

ISBN 0-7700-0310-9

PRINTED AND BOUND IN CANADA
BY THE RYERSON PRESS

CONTENTS

[handwritten marginal note at top: "If this def. of 'convent. novel' is 19th c. In 20th c. novel a lot of other things & rightly so — why stick with 20th c. def.?"]

I

It is perhaps significant that the most perceptive reviews which followed the publication of *The Second Scroll* in 1951 were more convinced of its cultural importance than of its merits as a novel. The immediate problem was to decide by what standard this original and unusual work, which deals with the persecution of the Jews and their redemption in the nation of Israel, ought to be judged, since it made virtually no pretence to be a conventional novel with realistic plot and fully rounded characterization.

[handwritten marginal note: "No — both"]

North American Jewish critics generally agreed that the book was a significant attempt to explore the Jewish experience in the twentieth century and in all times and places. Allen Mendelbaum wrote in *Commentary*:

The present work by A. M. Klein is novel, travel book, personal memoir, history-biography of the Jew as wanderer, confession of faith and work of love. This multiplicity marks the ambitiousness of *The Second Scroll* and its impressiveness: no other Jewish writer in English has attempted to give symbolic—as against episodic—form to so much Jewish experience.

[handwritten marginal note: "What about while in diders ... & you remove 'Jewish' from some"]

Harvey Swados, writing in *The Nation,* took a similar line. *The Second Scroll* was, he felt, "the most profoundly creative summation of the Jewish condition by a Jewish man of letters since the European Catastrophe."[1]

---

[1] "A Work of Splendor," The Nation, Nov. 3, 1951, 379.

Maurice Samuel, in his review for *Jewish Frontier,* suggested further that *The Second Scroll* was perhaps the beginning of a real Jewish-American literature:

We shall never have in America a Jewish culture, regionaliste, indigenous, and yet in our tradition, if we think of separation and privacy. We shall have it, if at all, only as a consequence of complete acceptance of our locale. A Jewish culture in America can exist only in symbiosis with an American culture. . . .

The literary idiom of that Jewish culture in the west is yet to be created; or let me say that it is in process of creation in *The Second Scroll.*

This is high praise and gives some indication of the book's importance for a Jew. But none of these Jewish American critics seems to have reflected that the cosmopolitan reach and poetic power of Klein's fable of Israel might have something to do with the fact that he is a Canadian. After all, no American Jew has attempted to create such a comprehensive work.

Malcolm Ross's comments in *The Canadian Forum* may somewhat restore the balance. He suggests something of the nature of Klein's Canadianism when he asserts that the literary tradition that is native to Canada is inescapably cosmopolitan, since Canadians are "a uniquely structured people with multi-dimensional cultural possibilities." In his poetry, Dr. Ross proceeds, "Klein has come close to creating the archetypal Canadian pattern—a dense organic fusion of traditional idiom, ancient myth and cult, the contrapuntal dialectic of our French-English relationship, the sophisticated technical reach of man alive in this age and in whom all ages are alive." Klein, the twentieth-century poet of the people Israel, is the voice of Canada as well.

How can this be? What sort of novel is *The Second Scroll*? What is Canadian about it?

Malcolm Ross is a good guide in these matters. Let us

stay with him for the moment, and consider this attempt at a brief general description of the book:

The novel, Klein's first, is experimental in form, complex in theme. It is the story of a quest at once personal, communal and spiritual. The method is that of analogy and is therefore of a piece with the patterning of diverse and seemingly discontinuous facts of experience characteristic of Klein's best poetry. Obviously, Klein has been schooled by Joyce but, perhaps because of the clear unequivocal religious affirmation of this novel, one is reminded not so much of Joyce as of Dante. The inferno of pogrom gives way in turn to purgatorial quest, to a realization of the Earthly Paradise of the new Jerusalem, even to a prospect of the universal and eternal.

Klein hoped in the late forties to write a book about Joyce, and he had made use of Dante in some of his earliest poetry. Both influences were likely to lead him in the direction of poetic myth or allegorical fable. *Ulysses, The Divine Comedy* and *The Second Scroll* have in common the archetypal pattern of the personal odyssey that holds spiritual significances for mankind at large. In Klein's treatment of Zionism Jewish literature takes its place in western literature as a whole.

Where then is the book's Canadianism? The answer must be that this lies, paradoxically, in its very assumption of universality. A Canadian is aware, and this is true for any sensitive Canadian, though especially so for a Jew, that his national character is fluid and tentative, that he lives, on one level, in an international situation. Canada is a country of two languages and at least five intense and mutually exclusive regionalisms, a land in which each racial group holds firmly to its own heritage from the old world but is also confronted with those of other groups. This situation can and does produce both petty exclusivism and a wide tolerance embodied in the general agreement to disagree. As Edmund Wilson and other foreign

Marshall seems to be just writing footnotes to Ross

observers have noted, Canada has never been and could not be a melting pot. It has too many divisions and too many separate and distinct ties to Europe, the British Commonwealth and the United States. It is necessarily a heterogeneous society.

Malcolm Ross stresses the most positive aspect of this:

Ross

Talmud and Torah take their place in our pattern beside the Book of Common Prayer, the Missal, the Institutes. We are enriched. And we acknowledge that the racial memories of our multi-dimensional culture are much too deep and broad to be filled by Cartier and Wolfe and the U.E. Loyalists. It is not the item but the *pattern* which is Canadian. As persons we live by various and separate spiritual inheritances and loyalties and we preserve our differences. But at another level, as Canadians, we take our life from the fruitful collision and interpretation of many inheritances. And thus we grow.

It is possible (though not, by any means, inevitable) that at this stage in our cultural development—a stage of flux in the developing national consciousness roughly comparable to the stage that produced Hawthorne, Melville and Whitman in the United States—that the fable is a more effective vehicle than the realistic novel for the Canadian writer's distinctive attempt to present a significant exploration of the human condition. As D. H. Lawrence perceived the symbolic meaning of the literature of nineteenth-century America, so D. G. Jones has traced some of the symbolic patterns that have informed our own early literature in his article "The Sleeping Giant" (*Canadian Literature* No. 26). Certainly, one can see elements of romance and allegory in even the most "realistic" novels of Callaghan, MacLennan, Buckler, Raddall and Ross. Certain figures— the questing artist who shapes or transfigures the landscape, the wandering hero, the enduring and maturing woman—occur again and again. They do in many ages and many literatures, of course, but they are especially appro-

Canada now like US late 19thc

priate and useful in the early stages of cultural self-discovery. Douglas LePan, himself the author of a novel of highly charged poetic symbolism, *The Deserter*, speaks of the usefulness for the Canadian writer of an attempt at expression "in terms of what happens in an anonymous setting to an anonymous, or virtually anonymous, hero" in order to produce "a result of almost universal luminosity which can be understood anywhere." He considers this a valid mode of expression because of the writer's consciousness that "one can in fact, be almost anyone and still be a Canadian; and to be a Canadian is to have a passport to the whole world."[2] Thus the international development of the symbolic novel in the twentieth century has been of special use to Canadian writers striving to make sense of the multi-dimensional Canadian experience—not only Burroughs and Barth but Klein's *Second Scroll* (and behind it Joyce) lead to *Beautiful Losers* (with its multi-racial, multi-dimensional single protagonist). In Canada nationalism is internationalism.

I have heard Mr. LePan remark that he felt Jewish-Canadian writers were in a uniquely favourable cultural position to realize the possibilities of the Canadian situation. As an unusually stable and cohesive group related to larger cultural entities both inside and outside of Canada, the Jews are, in a sense, the most Canadian of Canadians. We should not be surprised then that the vision at the heart of all Klein's work is one of unity in diversity. For this is something eminently Canadian.

II

The young Klein's "Canadian" eclecticism was remarked upon by his first serious critic, W. E. Collin, in 1936: "It is a charming art which mingles East and West, Hebrew lyric, Arthurian lay, Provençal *alba*, Gallician *cantigas de*

---

[2]Douglas LePan, "The Dilemma of the Canadian Author," *The Atlantic Monthly*, CCXIV (1964), 164.

amigo, and weaves a dream of fair women with a polyglot woof of many-coloured silks." Klein's exiled lovers, asserted Collin, would always long for Zion, but would never go there "because they cannot give their whole souls to Israel." On the other hand, Ludwig Lewisohn, in his introduction to Klein's first collection, *Hath Not A Jew* (1940), felt that it was his fidelity to his Jewish heritage that made Klein "the only Jew who has ever contributed a new note of style, of expression, of creative enlargement to the poetry of [the English] tongue." This is a large claim. Moreover, it is indisputable that Klein's early style owes as much to the great Elizabethans as to the Jewish world. As Louis Dudek later remarked, he settled on Elizabethan diction as a medium for Hebrew passion. It is the fusion of Jewish attitudes and subject-matter with an archaic English idiom that is remarkable, if not wholly admirable, in the early poems.

Hath Not A Jew is made up, for the most part, of Klein's very early poems, most of them written in the late Twenties and early Thirties. He excluded from this book his poems of social protest written in the middle and late Thirties, and was mildly criticized for this by Leon Edel in *Poetry.* "These poems," Mr. Edel observed, "were close to the modern ghetto and therefore close to life; they were filled with witty observations and a delightful mixture of the real and the fantastic; they were pungent, vigorous and above all true." Most later critics have disliked these uncollected poems of Klein's second period, but Miriam Waddington has recently sought to revive interest in them. It seems to me that, whatever their intrinsic worth, these poems represent a significant development in Klein's work. His early optimism disappears, and there is a radical change in his attitudes. The search for self and for God, a major concern in his earliest and latest work, seems in the Thirties a hopeless luxury in an evil and unjust world where one is hard put to get enough to eat. There may very well be no God to find; it may be the world is moved only by force and greed. Klein is unable to offer any creative solution for the social ills he describes, and he has nothing now to say about the restoration of Israel as a solution for Jewry's troubles.

This loss of the faith, firmly based in Judaism but universal in its potential, that is at the core of both Klein's early poetry and *The Second Scroll* (a loss paralleled in the latter work by Melech's lapse into communism) was apparently brought about by the atrocities of fascism in Europe and the sufferings of the great Depression in North America. The latter more especially seem to have brought Klein out of the apparently inadequate shelter of his particular tradition and forced him to face the urban world of Montreal in which he had to live. This process was eventually to have a beneficial effect on his poetry when he was able to reconcile his first instincts about the world with his deepening awareness of the importance of material needs and his growing realization that social groups other than Jewry are created and sustained for similar purposes. Thus his original, rather academic ecumenicism, always dependent upon a creative enlargement of basic human sympathies, was made more meaningful and complete.

I do not know whether or not Klein was impressed by Leon Edel's complaint that the stoicism of *Hath Not A Jew* left no room for "eloquent rebellion," but it is interesting that in the years of the Second World War his poems became at once less bitter and more defiant. There is, perhaps, a refreshing simplicity about a conflict joined. The poet of *The Hitleriad* (1944) cannot, whatever his faults, be accused of a passive stoicism or of "closing his eyes and folding his hands and dreaming sweet dreams of a glamorous ghetto." As E. J. Pratt expressed it, the "subject has pulled the threnodist away from the wall of lamentation and placed the satirist in a colosseum with a grenade in his hand and a good round curse on his lips." It is interesting that Pratt, considered the leading Canadian poet of the time, spoke kindly of this crude satire, which could,

I think, only have been written and published in wartime. Irving Layton went so far as to call the poem "a landmark in our rapidly growing national literature," noting, however, that the attempt to humanize the Nazis (by concentrating on Goebbels' halitosis or Streicher's hefty rear) in order to satirize them could not be considered an appropriate tactic.[3] F. Cudworth Flint's brief and objective dismissal of the poem is in rather interesting contrast to the apparent necessity for Canadians such as Pratt, Layton and E. K. Brown to defend it.

The Hitleriad concludes with the naive belief that Hitler's destruction will signify the beginning of a Messianic era. However, the poem's attempts to explain the phenomenon of Hitler are largely inadequate, presumably because Klein was incapable of feeling at one with such a man. Hitler was beyond his understanding. Thus he resorted to the expedient, essentially false to his vision of the world's oneness, of considering Hitler as some sort of subhuman freak or moron, a virtual golem. He has little insight into the nature of evil, as Irving Layton has observed in another context. He would have it something that is ultimately illusory and trivial. But one cannot use caricature to deal with profound evil. The burning of Rotterdam is not a piece of bureaucratic pomposity. There may be a sense in which Hitler was the "total bigness of/ All little men," but few little men could do what he did. Chaplin runs into the same difficulty as Klein in *The Great Dictator;* Brecht perhaps solved it by translating his Hitler to Chicago and making him a comic-strip gangster in *The Irresistible Rise of Arturo Ui.*

In his review of *Poems* (1944) Irving Layton pinpoints Klein's major weakness when he suggests that the "deeper note," the full realization of man's (i.e. one's own) incorrigible nature is usually lacking in Klein's questioning of the Deity. He expects, as he did in his earliest ballads of miracles and wonders, a coming time of the Messiah when

[3]*First Statement*, Vol. II, No. 9, Oct.-Nov. 1944.

original sin (or, more properly, human aggression) will be eliminated (Miriam Waddington has suggested that such a notion as original sin probably never held any validity for him in any case), and Eden restored on earth. John Sutherland, the first critic to apply very rigorous standards to Klein's early work, goes so far as to say (mistakenly, in my opinion) that the young Klein, whose children's poems with their chassidic gaiety he found very charming, seemed incapable of expressing a serious idea or "even a serious emotion" in poetry.

Klein believed that man would "don his godliness." But man's "godliness," his brief and fleeting vision of the common lot of all his brethren, is a personal transcendence of human suffering and serves the psychological function of reconciling him to the inevitable. For the human condition is inescapable, even when suffering is minimized by awareness and sympathy. Human selfishness and human conflict are inherent in human need for personal integrity. Klein ignores this even when he expresses the desire to be part of the One and yet to contain within oneself all of experience. Man's wish to be the One generates both what he calls good and what he calls evil. For it blends sympathy and egoism, as D. H. Lawrence observed of Whitman. A greater awareness of this might have made Klein's vision of unity more profound.

For the tendency of his work is toward a greater awareness of the facts of life. In *The Rocking Chair* Klein accepts his loss of innocence even when he cannot comprehend its necessity. But his conception of Israel as the road back to Eden places too heavy a burden on that beleaguered and struggling nation-state. One does not have to agree with Kenneth Rexroth's criticism of Martin Buber's zionism to see that it raises important issues which Klein will not raise in *The Second Scroll*. Rexroth writes:

Buber tries hard to etherealize both the Zionist movement and the State of Israel. He considers this the redemptive role of prophecy, the continual confrontation of the secular

state with the transcendental demands of an intention, a
destination, beyond the world. This may give him comfort,
but it does not alter the facts. Zionism remains an
imperialist maneuver, invented by Napoleon and taken
over by the British and used with considerable effective-
ness in the First World War. Israel remains the final outcome of this maneuver, an aggressive nationalist State
founded on invasion and war, and perpetuated by con-
scription of both girls and boys and by the militarization
of wide sections of life.[4]

One can only answer that Klein's Israel, like his chassidic
dream-kingdom of Jewish lore, is a state of mind, and,
more than this, a modern Canadian Jew's rediscovery of
his heritage in palpable form. In celebrating the renewal
of the Hebrew land and culture he ignores the political
and moral issues raised by Rexroth. In his defence it may
be said that his best work expresses the tension between
the real and the ideal, and reveals a deep desire for fusion
and incarnation. He is not so innocent as he sometimes
seems.

Klein's utopianism is evident in the very significant
poem of the war years that eventually became Gloss Aleph
in The Second Scroll. In "Autobiographical" the poet bids
farewell to his innocent and enchanted childhood. He
casts his eyes backward, dwelling as he does elsewhere on
the first discovery of nature. He looks forward as well,
however, for his continuing quest is implicit in the statement that he still seeks a "fabled city." This is the first
poem in which he depicts with very much affection Montreal, the real "jargoning city" itself, and he is to picture it
thus again in The Rocking Chair. John Sutherland has
written: "The real scene has displaced the fabled city, as
the power to describe it has triumphed over the knack of
transforming it into a romantic dream"; but this is not
entirely the case since Klein is to invest Montreal with the

[4]Kenneth Rexroth, Bird in the Bush (New York: New Directions, 1947),
132-33.

same magic he gave to the fabled city of Jewish lore. Beyond this, he is to seek his fabled city in Israel, to end his quest in the holy city of Safed, and then to return forever to Montreal. He is to appreciate the marvels of two cities, Rome and Casablanca (i.e. Christianity and Islam), but is to go on to Safed, and to return, spiritually refreshed, to Montreal. All are fabled cities, points in his journey.

Thus this poem, firmly based in his home city, appears to be central in his development. It looks backward to the glamorous ghetto of traditions and dreams and forward to the full physical realization both of Montreal and of Israel. By expressing his first dreams in the physical depiction of these realities Klein the artist is again able, as Melech was, to make the Word will. In the poems of the "Canadian" period this Zionist dreamer brings his "Jewish" insights into the nature of minority groups and cultural co-existence to the study (and, indeed, the creation) of his other native country.

III

It is act

> and symbol, symbol of this static folk
> which moves in segments, and returns to base—
> a sunken pendulum: *invoke, revoke;*
> loosed yon, leashed hither, motion on no space.
> O, like some Anjou ballad, all refrain,
> which turns about its longing, and seems to move
> to make a pleasure out of repeated pain,
> its music moves, as if always back to a first love.

What is it that happens when a routine, even somewhat sentimental and banal piece of work by a talented poet transcends itself in this extraordinary way? In "The Rocking Chair" the deliberate and somewhat corny folksiness of the first two stanzas unexpectedly gives way to the resonance of the conclusion. Margaret Avison found such specifically Canadian poems as this "a little dreary" and felt the real excitement of Klein's verse emerged when, in a poem such as "Grain Elevator," he was able to "speak of Canada and sound the note that wakens vibrations through all times and places." Surely this happens as well in the conclusion of "The Rocking Chair": one perceives that French Canada, like Canada itself, is, despite its introversion, a nation with invisible cultural boundaries, a microcosm in the macrocosm. The last few lines are equally expressive of the mature Klein's own emotional and intellectual rhythm, his return to his first, sustaining instincts about his place in the worlds of nature and society, and of the general recurrence of basic values in the life of the French-Canadian, the Jewish and, indeed, the whole Western cultural tradition. The Anjou ballad and the rocking chair partake equally of the circular movement of earth's relenting and recurring life. It is, then, the imaginative reach of the passage, powerfully reinforced by sound and rhythm, that makes it so effective.

"To make a pleasure out of repeated pain." There is an undercurrent here, perhaps a key to Klein's psychology. We are reminded both of the poet whose kingdom shines at the bottom of the sea and of the "ambiguity" of the human situation, the precarious nature of man's participation in divinity, as it is expressed in Gloss Gimel. One can perhaps trace this paradox of painful pleasure in the submergence of the individual in the eternal pattern back to the ideas of Spinoza as they are expressed in "Out of the Pulver and the Polished Lens" (Milton Wilson has suggested that this very early poem might easily be called "Portrait of Spinoza as Landscape").

In this poem, as in "Portrait of the Poet as Landscape," Klein searches for context and thus for identity by seeking God as the principle of order in the natural universe. The artist, "solitary man," defines himself by naming and praising the parts of the One to which all belong. Within the One individual man is nothing, a fragment praying unto perfection, but he is also everything since he partakes too in the common divinity of creation. Death is ultimately defeated by the permanence of life in God's one creation.

Libby Benedict has aptly written that Klein's humility is "not humility at all because it merges with the cosmos and is therefore at once the apotheosis of pride, is one of the secret springs of Jewish endurance."[5] Klein himself notes this peculiarly Jewish way of coming to God in "Dance Chassidic":

> Thus let the soul be cast from pride, gesticulating
> Into humility, and from humility
> Into the pride divine, so alternating
> Until pride and humility be one,
> Until above the Jews, above the Scroll, above the
>   Cherubim,
> There broods the Immanence of Him . . . .

The humility that is pride is a concept related to the idea that the dot or ghetto can become a circle. The small may grow very large because the same One underlies all individual things. Even more straightforward than Melech's recapitulation of the credos of Maimonides in *The Second Scroll,* Klein's "one creed" is

> A simple sentence broken by no commas
> ("Design for Mediaeval Tapestry")

And yet, the individual man is subject to disease and death, and this painful knowledge engenders the intense frustration and feelings of aggression that cause man's inhumanity to man. This seems to me the only explanation the mature Klein is able to offer (even implicitly) for the spectacle of the descent of his godlike man to bestial cruelty in the Nazi camps:

They would be like gods; but since the godlike touch of creation was not theirs, like gods would they be in destructions. To kill wantonly, arrogantly, to determine that another's term is fulfilled—with impunity to do these things and be deemed therefore gods—such were their vain imaginings, the bouquet and flavour of their drink. It was the sin against our incarnate universality. Comes then Michelangelo to teach us that he who spills but a drop of the ocean of our consanguinity exsanguinates himself and stands before heaven by that much blanched, a leper; that such beginnings have terrible ends; it is the first murder that is difficult: and that the single gout released sets cataracts of carnage on to flood.

If murder is a perversion of divine creativity, then the murderer loses his divinity (i.e. his humanity) to become a beast. It is the imaginative failure to envision the One, to accept that even in decay he contributes to the One, that has driven him to this pass. He must learn to make a pleasure of repeated pain by accepting his own decline and death in order to rejoice in the larger Life.

Gloss Gimel is perhaps Klein's final attempt to resolve the mystery of evil within his One universe. Michelangelo's Sistine masterpiece is divinely inspired and prophetic, "the parable of the species", "the weighted animate corpus of humanity", "a great psalter psalmodizing the beauty and vigour and worth of the races of mankind." It is thus a book in which Klein is able to read the enigma of human history, and to perceive the glory and the terror of human possibility:

High and central in the chapel's empyrean the throned twenty bear down with an almost palpable imminence. Young men, handsome and marvellously sinewed, wonderful in their proportions, they are the prototype of the human kind; and whether face-to-face conversant or januarial back-to-back, or in their serpentinings muscle-rippled, there is upon them everywhere the glory of God's accolade. Brooding nudities, they are themselves like gods. Long-limbed, Atlas-shouldered, lyre-chested, each body is a song echoing the Creator's voice. *Fiat!* The dew of paradise is still upon them, they are ichor-fresh, ambrosia-scented; their gaze is Eden-rapt, all are adonic, almost adonaic! It is also to be seen that they know themselves earthlings, earthlings involved in concatenations far from celestial: group after group of them is perceived tangled in the circuit of these murderous medallions rolling before their feet, from which they recoil back horror-struck. Circle-rocked! Caught in these wheels the colour of dried blood, it is clear that they have an awareness of the ambiguity of their plight: their pristine unnamed felicity ever in peril of cicatrice and brand-mark. That peril, however, is below them, below their knees, and even there dark and obscured; about their countenances another aura reigns, the memory of the fingertouch, of God's lifegiving fingertouch, which through each pulsating vein and every quickened limb proclaims divine origins and makes of this adamic seraphic ceiling a pantheon of gods.

If man is divine, then murder is deicide, a crime that cannot succeed in its ultimate intention. The Jewish people could not utterly be destroyed, and indeed had been promised continuance and renewal. Thus, Melech's letter is affirmative in its conclusion, as is *The Second Scroll* itself.

What of the individual, though, the man who dies or merely suffers? "Portrait of the Poet as Landscape," in some respects more personal than Klein's two other major works, is also most qualified in its expression of ultimate triumph. Klein's poet shares (as all men must, to some degree) the minority psychology: he is a man especially anxious to transcend the ghetto of self, but who must nevertheless maintain an internal integrity. This tension generates his art. It is not so much possible fame (say, twenty years later, the fame of Leonard Cohen) as "stark infelicity," a desperate need for self-realization, that motivates him.

Therefore he seeds illusions. Look, he is
the nth Adam taking a green inventory
in world but scarcely uttered, naming, praising,
the flowering fiats in the meadow, the
syllabled fur, stars aspirate, the pollen
whose sweet collision sounds eternally.
For to praise

the world—he, solitary man—is breath
to him. Until it has been praised, that part
has not been. Item by exciting item—
air to his lungs, and pressured blood to his heart—
they are pulsated, and breathed, until they map
not the world's but his own body's chart!

Like the Walt Whitman of "A Child Went Forth," Klein's
poet attempts to capture through his senses the whole
external world of his experience, and thus become one
with it. This experience provides a context, a larger world
or extended "body" within which to define himself. Like
Whitman, Klein sees the poet as Adam the namer and
praiser, as the articulate voice of what all men feel. The
nth Adam is everyman.

Thus the poet's function is still of the highest use to
himself and to everyone else. If he is zero, his zero is a
garland, a halo, a circle capable of infinite expansion. If
he is nobody, he is nevertheless landscape (i.e. everybody).
He is still, despite the usurpations of the scientist, the
potential interpreter of the universe.

These are not mean ambitions. It is already something
merely to entertain them. Meanwhile, he
makes of his status as zero a rich garland,
a halo of his anonymity,
and lives alone, and in his secret shines
like phosphorus. At the bottom of the sea.

The suggestion of personal disappointment and even
tragedy is there, but the poet's achievement nevertheless

involves another defeat for Death. Physical death is not denied, but the "relenting and recurring life" of the world is re-affirmed each time that it is re-discovered and re-created in the poetic imagination. The activity of poetry is at once the search for and discovery of the self, the realization of union with the One, and the elimination of evil (which has its source, according to Klein, in the absence of this realization). Man forgets easily, and must struggle again and again to see the world whole.

IV

In some of his verses—"Annual Banquet: Chamber of Commerce"—he is in fact still at the point which Pound and Eliot reached in 1915. But in other poems he moves forward—almost touches something exciting and new. . . .

These experiments are nothing new in literature, since Whitman called the *Leaves of Grass* "a language experiment," and before him the *Lyrical Ballads, Paradise Lost,* and *The Fairie Queene* were also of this kind. Klein therefore is in a great tradition, and in good modern company. He has been doing something that Canada badly needs: making new things with old tools, discovering the vast possibilities of poetry.

(Louis Dudek, "A. M. Klein")

Nowadays, of course, one has to add William Carlos Williams and Charles Olson to Louis Dudek's list of those poets who have made notable experiments with language. This leads one immediately to the reflection that Klein strove, like Hopkins, Joyce, Auden and Dylan Thomas, to enrich the language of poetry with new (and appropriate) kinds of rhetoric and verbal play, not to purify it in the manner of Williams and some of his successors. Perhaps this difference was inevitable: Williams learned from Whitman to search for the American language, but what was the Canadian language? Could it best be expressed in the bilingual artifact of "Montreal"? Hardly. But where was it to be found?

On the one hand, there is the example of Spenser, who sought to re-affirm tradition with deliberate archaism, and, on the other (behind Whitman), the example of Words-worth, who felt poetry should employ "a selection of language really used by men." The early Klein, with his private pseudo-biblical or Elizabethan English, certainly opted for the former procedure. But what the later Klein does is more complex. He is at once more aware of the language actually spoken by his contemporaries and of the necessity to reconcile this with the language and idioms of his own variegated cultural context, i.e. his language must reflect the complexity of the "multi-dimensional" Canadian cultural possibility. This is especially evident in the poems of *The Rocking Chair* and in the diction and syntax of Gloss Gimel, as Miriam Waddington has demon-strated elsewhere.

In such a poem as "Lookout: Mount Royal" the occa-sional extravagance of language co-exists happily with "normal" speech and a "realistic" clarity of observation:

> . . . from the parapet make out
> beneath the green marine
> the discovered road, the hospital's romantic
> gables and roofs, and all the civic Euclid
> running through sunken parallels and lolling
> in diamond and square, then proud-pedantical
> with spire and dome
> making its way to the sought point, his home.
>
> home recognized: there: to be returned to—
>
> lets the full birdseye circle to the river,
> its singsong bridges, its mapmaker curves, its
> island with the two shades of green, meadow and wood;
> and circles round that water-tower'd coast;

then, to the remote rhapsodic mountains; then,
—and to be lost—
to clouds like white slow friendly animals
which all the afternoon across his eyes
will move their paced spaced footfalls.

Here the metaphors and similes, the combination adjectives, the alliteration, the occasional and internal rhymes
point to the experience of the "real" Montreal rather than
distracting the reader from it. Here is the clarity, the high
definition that was not achieved in "Montreal." The poem
somewhat resembles Auden's "Look, Stranger," but is, in
my opinion, much less affected in its technique. It is Klein
at his best.

What, finally, is Klein's importance to those who have
come after him? In the years of his tragic silence what can
we conclude about his published work? If it is true, as
Irving Layton has reportedly said, that the "economic,
social and cultural forces that produced the milieu out of
which had come the distinctive poetry of A. M. Klein,
Leonard Cohen and myself" are no longer operative, then
what has been the significance for the rest of Canada of that
very remarkable succession of poets?

It has always seemed to me that there were two main
streams (perhaps there are a thousand subsidiaries) in
modern Canadian poetry. These involve two approaches to
the act of poetic creation, two approaches to Canada. On
the one hand, the poet can begin with observation and
exploration, the facts of history, geography and society, and
make from them a pattern that may be meaningful—this
seems to me to be what happens in much of the poetry of
E. J. Pratt, Earle Birney and Alfred Purdy. This kind of
approach is easily reconciled with William Carlos Williams's search for a North American language and his
insistence on a definite sense of place, as the work of such
poets as Raymond Souster, Alden Nowlan, John Newlove
and George Bowering demonstrates. On the other hand,

the poet can begin with dream, with the inner life that expresses in its own way and with its own crazy logic the truth about the world. This seems to me to be the procedure of such poets as Klein, Layton, Cohen, James Reaney, Gwendolyn MacEwen and Margaret Atwood.

It is, of course, more a difference in emphasis than in essential purpose. Each poet strives in his own way for the centre where "the fact is the sweetest dream that labour knows." Klein began with exotic tales and fantasies based on Jewish cultural history and folklore but was able eventually to fuse this dream world with his external environment in *The Rocking Chair*. Similarly, Layton, in powerful surrealist visions like "The Improved Binoculars" and "Me, the P.M. and the Stars" was able to denounce the spiritual failures of Canadian society.

Klein has bequeathed to his successors the task of creating their country. The emphasis on space and landscape in "Grain Elevator" and "Portrait of the Poet as Landscape" is echoed in the work of Margaret Avison and Margaret Atwood. Klein's "nth Adam," the unacknowledged legislator of a new Canada of the spirit, may be found in the poems of Gwendolyn MacEwen and Joe Rosenblatt, and even in Cohen's *Beautiful Losers*. In fact, it is increasingly evident to this writer that the work of A. M. Klein, whatever its faults, is still of the first importance to us, and that Klein himself, because of the largeness of his concerns and the vitality and impassioned technical virtuosity of his best work, is the man who has come closer than any other Canadian poet to greatness.

TOM MARSHALL

Kingston, Ontario; London, England
May 1964—September 1969

The Spirit's Palestine

W. E. Collin

Reprinted from "The Spirit's Palestine" in Collin's The White Savannahs *(Toronto: The Macmillan Company of Canada, 1936), by permission of The Macmillan Company of Canada Limited.*

W. E. Collin's essays in The White Savannahs *have been called "over-written," and certainly Collin was excited by his writers, but such a description fails to do justice to his insights into his subject. Moreover, his was the first very serious essay to be devoted to Klein's work. Because of the Depression Klein (like most other Canadian poets of the time) had to wait some ten years before his first collection appeared. Collin suggests Klein's relationships to Jewish lore and to European literature, and the fruitful tension created in his work by these disparate influences. I have omitted some of his longer quotations from Klein's poems along with what seemed mere description rather than criticism.*

St. Lawrence Main and its tributary streets constitute the Ghetto, one of the three Jewish settlements in Montreal. It is a "warren of small stores and tumbling houses, where large red-faced butchers sire smaller butchers and the occasional poet." Leo Kennedy no doubt had a particular poet in mind when he wrote those lines. Do not infer that Abraham Moses Klein's father was a butcher—he was by profession really a potter—but rather that the poet might have been a butcher or a presser or a cutter or, more probably still, an orthodox rabbi if the soul of this

1

Jewish boy, as all his magnificent poetry and all his multi-
farious activities attest, had not been illumined, yea fired,
with a vision which will never let him rest: a vision of
emancipation. The outward and visible environment in
which he was reared may well be that described by
Kennedy: the Ghetto with its "shabby-derbied and round-
shouldered rabbonim twisting syllogistic thumbs at beard
level on many a crowded corner . . . with large silk and
velvet clad matrons ponderously shoving imported English
perambulators, laden till the springs squeak with one
chubby Yidel and the week-end's vegetables . . . with over-
barbered and under-read 'cavaliers' lurching in and out
of pool rooms and the back parlors of barber shops, where
craps and pinochle are grave pursuits . . . with the bright
white windows of bake shops offering strings of bagel and
loaves of shabbas broit . . . with the prosperous and noisy
delicatessens wafting out into the disturbed night their
mingled smells of herring, smoked meat, salami and swiss
cheese . . . while from the kosher restaurants with their
insistent window legends and blue mogen dovids, emerge
high and enervating odours of truly exquisite borscht,
stuffed miltz, and the all-encompassing, ultimately satisfying incense of pot roast chicken."[1] But the air the poet
breathes is not that. If Klein's parents had had money they
would have pushed him into the rabbinate;[2] as it is he
went through most of the prescribed readings for love.
He knows his Torah and Talmud and his Graetz. He
thoroughly assimilated what the history, literature and
rabbinical erudition of his race could offer his healthy and
inspired appetite. He lives partly on that and, in part, on
the cultural nourishment he obtained outside the Ghetto.
Klein's soul, without a doubt, is an ardent symbol of the
spiritual rebirth of the Jewish people; the resounding
anger and the prophetic vision, the impassioned lyricism
of his poetry witnesses to the depth and intensity of Israel's

---

[1] *The Jewish Standard*, Toronto, Sept. 30, 1932.
[2] He is now practising law in Montreal.

awakening to a realization of her ancient and splendid
destiny, yet one of the rare qualities his poetry possesses—
although it is not my intention to stress it unduly—is the
tone, the mature, the gentle tone due indisputably to a
power his soul acquired through intimate association with
the literatures of Europe. Klein will not let us forget this.
He gives us not only "Designs for Mediaeval Tapestry"
and the "Ballad of the Dancing Bear" but also the "XXII
Sonnets"; not only "Portraits of a Minyan"[3] and "Talisman in Seven Shreds"[4] but also the "Diary of Abraham
Segal, Poet"[5]—a long *sirventes* built to Eliot specifications,
reinforced at intervals by a line from Moréas or Mallarmé,
dramatized, it is true, by "gestures Hebraic" but at the
same time spiced with Chaucer and Shakespeare. The
various moods of the Jewish mind and its nostalgia are
tempered by an æsthetic attachment to Elizabeth and
Dante. The poet's pilgrimage to the Holy Land is through
a ghetto of bitter herbs for Love's sweet sake.

> O love casts roses beneath broken shoes,
> And paves this ghetto street with burnished
> gold.[6]

Chivalry, at any rate the age of chivalry, is a purely
Western phenomenon sprung from the soil of European
Christian culture.

"As a nation," says Klein, speaking of his own people,
"we were forced to suffer eighteen centuries of stunned
amazement before we realized that God helps those who
help themselves."[7] After the pogroms of 1880 in Russia
Dr. Leo Pinsker published his Zionist classic, *Auto-
Emancipation,* which has some effect in recalling the Jews
from their "stunned amazement" and inciting them to act.

[3] *Menorah Journal*, Oct., 1929.
[4] *Ibid.*, July, 1932.
[5] *The Canadian Forum*, May, 1932.
[6] "Gestures Hebraic."
[7] *The Judaean*, Montreal, Nov., 1931.

"Among the living nations of the earth," wrote Pinsker,[8] "the Jews occupy the position of a nation long since dead. The whole world saw in this people the uncanny form of one of the dead walking among the living." Klein tilts his lance against all forms of death; he will kill death and all her ministers—in the name of life. Simply to frame some concept by which our minds might grasp the unity in Klein's material we may regard his poetry as the illustration of a knightly outlook on life and all that outlook implies. Zionism is a vision of a return to, and life in, Palestine, the realization of which will lead the poet to war on false prophets, to seek his ship and ultimately—where?

The ghetto is crowded with false prophets who connive with expediency or resign themselves, who keep the letter of the law without raising a finger to remedy their condition, who rant at God, who have lost the spirit of the Jewish epics. There are streets full of them in the "Ballad of the Dancing Bear" and "Ave Atque Vale"; and it is from the depths of moral turpitude as well as bricks and mortar in the present year of grace that Klein cries "out of a pit of perpendiculars." He faces them all; the tone with which he treats them makes clear the essential differences between his nature and F. R. Scott's. Scott's ironical mood expressed itself in satire which at best was hardly more than a sneer. . . .

Passages of Klein's writing take us back through Elizabethan drama to the old Hebrew epic. . . . We are in a mood now and hear a language we never felt or heard in Scott. This dramatic realism and prophetic wrath, this combination of Shakespeare and Jeremiah, of blood and brain, is entirely new to us and entirely Klein's. His brother poets have no prophets, no persecution of epic proportions, therefore no anger. Neither have they phylacteries or many-branched candelabra or unleavened bread; neither have they spices, figs, dates or "toothsome" almonds,

---

[8]Quoted by Klein.

ointments or choicest ornaments, sweet wine or gold from
Ophir. But let us not be dupes of an alluring Orientalism
or exotic religious ritual; let us not gape indecorously at
these quinquiremes from Nineveh. Let us move warily
through the tapestries of Oriental splendour and accustom
our eyes to the hangings on the walls and not be afraid of
the flutter near the cushioned carved head of a soft couch.
We have met her before, this beautiful Shoshannah who
is reclining there, even if she have "jet-black hair" and lips
"as red as is the core of ripe pomegranates." She is the
"fairest daughter of fair Lebanon":

> Thy smile is like the whiteness of the tusk
>   Of ivory, my darling one, and thy
> Sweet breath is as a waft of powdered musk
>   Within a garden when a wind doth sigh . . .
> Thy hair is like the coolness of the dusk,[9]

but, rare phenomenon, she is not the Shulamite. Behind
the "algum-casemented window" where she dreams of a
caravanserai and a Prince who will climb her high lattice
wall and carry her away, she is neither the Shulamite nor
the Lady of Shalott but related to both; she will not miss
the fields of barley and of rye because she will cultivate
them where she is in Lebanon. It is a charming art which
mingles East and West, Hebrew lyric, Arthurian lay,
Provencal *alba*, Gallician *cantigas de amigo*, and weaves a
dream of fair women with a polyglot woof of many-
coloured silks. "Legend of Lebanon" is the dream of a
poet who is at once a Zionist and a Christian knight.

To anathematize the false prophets Klein had to ha-
rangue them in the "ghetto-lanes of Prague" and Montreal;
to fight the oppressor he had to encounter baron and
burgher in Poland and Russia; to probe the misery into
which Jewry had sunk he had to grovel in Central Euro-

---

[9] "Legend of Lebanon," *The Jewish Standard*, Apr. 14, 1933.

pean villages after a pogrom when it was most hideous
and revolting. But what is this?

> Shoshannah, sweet Shoshannah, lovely one,
> .   .   .   .
> Awake, arise.

Not a forgotten spring-song of the great wise king, not a
serenade that Romeo might have crooned, but the love-
song of an exile gazing out of ghetto-lanes towards orange-
groves and distant Palestinian skies embowering home and
love.

From Zionist literature, from the writings of Martin
Buber perhaps more especially, Klein's mind grasped the
concept of a People as a succession of generations growing
up and propagating their kind in harmony, as it were,
with the great cyclic rhythm of nature. The ghetto Jews
have a calendar but they have not life. Nature is life, the
earth is life. As a contrast to the No-Land of exile, sterile
and hopeless, there is a land where the calendar is blended
with the natural life of the People. That is the vision of a
Zionist in whose heart is rooted the blended notion of land
and home—not a communist complex but an historical
belief that God gave the land to His people. This Zionist
outlook produced such poems as "Cargo"—fruits and
prayer-shawls and Torah rolls from Jaffa—and "Sonnet
XII."

As the years go by much of Klein's satirical and prophetic verse may lose its savour but the sonnets have an
abiding beauty. It is to them that we shall return as to an
inner chamber incensed with the tenderness, humility and
passion of a poet's soul; passion which still has sovereign
power, yet disciplined by study, enriched by learning,
gentle and strong.

> I rise from dreams
> Of you beside me on a garden lawn.[10]

---

[10]"Sonnet XIX."

Shelley, yes; but passing on we hear of an *aube* and *envoy* and *serenade* and realize that we are at the day-spring of the sonnet—far away beyond the nature sonnets of Lampman and Wordsworth—at the golden dawn in Italy. We think of Rossetti's love-songs and translations and, through them, of the immortal *Vita Nuova*.

There are evidences of the beginning of that New Life in "Sonnet XX." In a restaurant with his literati friends, "Platos exhaling smoke from cigarettes," "calling one another asses" and "shouting their love for the working-classes," he "toys with a blank menu and a pen" which scribbles:

L'amor che move il sole e l'altre stelle.

—the unforgettable line which closes the Divine Comedy. Is that not the sort of anecdote we should treasure if it concerned an Elizabethan coffee-shop or a Florentine street-meeting of Dante with Guido and Cino or Beatrice? The poet's pen might have scribbled another line:

Voi che, intendendo, il terzo ciel movete,

—you who, by your understanding or love, move the third heaven, that over which the star of Venus rules; the star that Dante saw filling the Orient of his Purgatory with joy and hope. The line seems to have been Dante's favourite since he repeats it several times and notably in the sonnet which Klein may have had in mind when he wrote:

Seventy regal moons, with clouds as train,
Have climbed the marble staircase of the sky,
Since we in homage first cried "Suzerain,
Accept thy lieges."[11]

---

[11]"Sonnet IV."

Who is this feudal lady, this "Suzerain" to whom the lovers render homage? She is the regnant moon; in the poet's third heaven Queen of Love.

> If there will be a moon to-night, arise,
> Put on your loveliest dress, and take the road
> That leads to mountains pivoting the skies.
> Regard the moon. Though at the antipode,
> And I upon these lowlands, am as far,
> Though I be miles from you, the moon, a mirror,
> Silvered and framed in many an angled star,
> Will smile your smile, and I will know you nearer.
> But if the moon still lingers in Cathay
> Or hangs caught in the branches of some tree,
> Or has been splintered by a comet-spray,
> Or lies drowned at the bottom of the sea,—
> Why, I will choose a hill, and sit on grass,
> And think of fate, and sigh, Alas! Alas! . . .[12]

Is there not a resemblance of Beatrice in that notion of reflected splendour, in that mirror-moon which smiles her smile? Did ever poet write a more beautiful "letter" to his beloved? Did Donne or Dante by whatsoever planetary mechanism render absence so physically sensible? Or troubadour sigh so hopelessly, deprived of his Lady's smile? But let her smile, then from her visage emanates the spirit of love, as when Beatrice moved her lips and said to the lover's soul: "Sospira." The smile, the sigh, the humble and charming attitude, the nostalgia, the incantation of the Tuscan school are all there, and a delicacy of feeling not anticipated in the satires. The technical significance of the sonnets is that a sweet singer of the lineage of David has tried to recapture the "dolce stil nuovo" for Canadian poetry.

Amor e cor gentil sono una cosa

---

[12]"Letters to One Absent."

is the definition of Klein's sensibility: love in a gentle heart.

> Would that three centuries past had seen us born!
> When gallants brought a continent on a chart
> To turreted ladies waiting their return.
> Then had my gifts to you declared my heart![13]

His attitude to his Lady is just that, whether as a Knight in shining armour, "unsullied, clean," offering precious gifts to his high-born Lady or as

> a humble thin-voiced Jew
> Hawking old clo'es in ghetto lanes, for you.

"Even," he says,

> Even if your heart were stone
> I would be its moss. . . .[14]

A twentieth-century troubadour, whose *terra lonhdana*[15] is at the antipode yet close as breathing, blends with love all the waking and warm emotions of spring blooms and summer suns. Winter and death he cannot bear. . . .

> O my beloved, do not sorrow thus.
> The moon has lost no lustre, and the sun
> No sunlight.[16]

Yet, like a parfait knight, he feels another's sorrow:

> Where shall I find choice words to mention
>   Sorrow
> That Sorrow may not be a pain to you?
>   . . . .

---

[13]"Sonnet VI."
[14]"Assurance."
[15]Jaufre Rudel: "Quan lo rius de la fontana."
[16]"Five Weapons against Death," *Menorah Journal*, Jan. 1929.

> Where shall I find such delicate, such tender
> Phrases as will slide off your heart, and not
> Open the wound that I had said had vanished?
> Where shall I find that soft word, that mild
>   thought?[17]

His vision of a Resurrection is awaking to "hear you weeping overhead." Death to him is the usurpation of powers and thrones by maggots, he wants to be alive: Spring is the season of his "perennial love-madnesses."

If we describe the style of the sonnets as feudal and Elizabethan—and there is no mistaking the ring of these lines:

> His face is as an ancient palimpsest
> Where tears have blurred the versions of a sorrow,
> Have blurred the varied versions of a sorrow,
> And blurring, made it all more manifest. . . .[18]

—we have taken no account of the vision, the vision which illumines all the domestic objects in the Jewish home and makes the poet's heart leap among almond-blossoms and golden oranges crying: "Jerusalem, next year!"

Hearing the "still small voice" beckoning intempestively they will start "from out the sleep assailing them" and mumble, perhaps a little crusty: "I will arise and go now." But once aroused to the present reality beyond the windowpanes they will exclaim:

> These northern stars are scarabs in my eyes.
> Not any longer can I suffer them. . . .[19]

If I were a Zionist I would hang those georgics in my study and read them every day. As it is I sit in admiration of that sonnet, its tone, and the perfect artistry of the first line:

> These northern stars are scarabs in my eyes.

---

[17]"Where shall I find Choice Words?"
[18]"Portrait."
[19]"Sonnet XII."

These "northern stars" and those "scarabs" have a magic power of evocation and together make an optically balanced picture. The very things that were indigenous in Scott, his very own, and which he wished to keep fresh and chaste, "unsullied" by Greek or Roman cult,[20] the "northern stars" of Canada have become symbols of an alien land in which a poet suffers and cannot stay. "Make ready to board ship," he calls to his beloved, "we will arise and seek the towers of Jerusalem." Let us watch them go.

On this summer morning the waters of the St. Lawrence and the hills beyond are bathed in the glory of a dawn which has put the northern stars to flight. An ocean liner is throbbing at the wharf taking on passengers and baggage for Tel Aviv. Groups of Zionists are disappearing over the hill towards the boat, while Ludwig Lewisohn and Martin Buber and Edmond Fleg are yet to come. Some of the lovers are chatting under the trees regardless of the dew upon their *escarpins,* perhaps oblivious of the cardinal's fiery call, while two, whose going has brought us here, have stopped upon the brink and turned their heads to say farewell. They will always stay like that, with their heads turned, and never go They are returning to Palestine and will never get there; because they cannot give their whole souls to Israel. The lure of Western culture creates a poignant problem in their consciences and casts a veil of melancholy over their faces, for it is man's spirit that yearneth. Dante wished that he could be carried off as if by enchantment and put upon a boat to sail away with Beatrice and his friends and spend the days talking of love. The Ideal boat, outward bound on this summer day for Cythera and the spirit's Palestine, responds to the same emotions through all the ages of man's history. Silhouetted against the Oriental magnificence of Klein's poetry, these lovers will always linger on the hill, gently leaning on each other, as in a Watteau picture, their heads o'ercargoed with alien and knightly romance, their hearts with loon-cries from the northern lakes.

---

[20]"New Names."

Ludwig Lewisohn

Reprinted, by permission, from Hath Not a Jew *by A. M. Klein, published by Behrman House, Inc., New York, 1940.*

This foreword is chiefly notable for Ludwig Lewisohn's apparent belief that Klein was destined to leave "great verse unto a little clan." A similar notion is expressed ten years later by Maurice Samuel when he declares that the literary idiom of a Jewish culture in the West is "in process of creation" in the The Second Scroll.

It is several years ago now that there began to appear in one or two not very conspicuous periodicals, poems signed Abraham M. Klein that both refreshed and excited me. I had then no notion who Klein was, and it was to be some years before I was to learn that a young Montreal attorney was destined to be the first contributor of authentic Jewish poetry to the English language. This statement can be at once abbreviated and enlarged: the first Jew to contribute authentic poetry to the literatures of English speech. For until his appearance all or nearly all Jews writing verse in English (and there were few enough even of those) had sought to make themselves more or less indistinguishable from the non-Jewish poets. Hence none of these men and women had gone to that core and visceral center whence poetry springs, and had therefore had no substance of their own which, given the talent, they could have transformed into a personal and therefore, if only the personality was salient and rich enough, an ultimately universal form.

The matter sounds intricate and is really simple enough.

We are not born on the day of our birth; we are not abstract and unfathered creatures. As we are born into the use of a given language or of several given languages, so we are born into a group, a tradition, a religion, a set of memories and attitudes concerning love and death, man and God. We need not blindly accept our heritage; we may legitimately rebel against it. But he who blankly "represses" it, denies it, flees from it, cannot evidently be a poet. For deep and strong poetry is the concrete, as Goethe was never tired of declaring, that *becomes* the universal. That perishable thing which is only symbol is an immensely concrete, individualized thing—a thing that has taken generations to grow, to become itself, never a thing contrived and constructed or imitated. Only the poet who has a substance of his very own will be able to create a style of his very own. And so an apparent paradox becomes a necessary truth: Abraham Klein, the most Jewish poet who has ever used the English tongue, is the only Jew who has ever contributed a new note of style, of expression, of creative enlargement to the poetry of that tongue. He is a far better English poet than the Jewish poets who tried to be non-Jewish English poets. In high things and low, honesty is not only the best policy; it is the only policy that makes for life.

The thing was illustrated to me with almost amusing emphasis upon my next contact with Klein's work. In a volume of *The American Caravan* published some years ago, a poetic work of Abraham Klein was placed next to a group of poems by another young American Jew who is rather spectacularly in flight from his Jewishness and therefore from his authentic self and his authentic humanity. And this far from untalented young man wrote of inchoate images in borrowed manners. He had recourse to the latest eccentricities to veil the poverty of concrete meanings in his heart. Abraham Klein, on the other hand, did not have to be frightened of the great tradition of English poetry. For he had that substance and that power of passionate meaning within him, which could take that tradition and forge within it the magnificent "Design for Mediaeval Tapestry" an instrument of expression which none had ever used except himself:

> The wrath of people is like foam and lather
> Risen against us. Wherefore, Lord and why?
> The winds assemble; the cold and hot winds gather
>
> To scatter us. They do not heed our cry.
> The sun rises and leaps the red horizon,
> And like a bloodhound swoops across the sky.

Klein had the luck, of course, to be born into a family and into an environment in which the lore and tradition of our people were things so alive that the quiver of this aliveness, so tense that it can humourously turn upon itself, has accompanied all his years. Therefore he has been able to turn the Berditshever's cries to the Eternal concerning the fate of Israel, and the dark tragedies of the Crusades, and Chelm, the fabled town of fools and the Pesach Haggadah, and the legend of Prague, and the dances of Chassidim, and the humours and ruling passions of a *Minyan*, and the vision and life of Baruch Spinoza into some of the most authentic and exciting English poetry of our day. He knows the Talmudic sages great and small as he knows the men and women on Saint Lawrence Street in Montreal, and into his English poetic style, even to the wild wit and sparkle of his rhymes, he has transfused their ardors, their dreams, their exquisite goodness, their storming of the very courts of God.

Few modern poets have been able to utter more than a lyric cry. Or else they have sought a depersonalization in the mass which is and must be the death of poetry. Klein occupies the classic middle station within which all important literature has hitherto been produced. As the Greek poets, according to Keats, left "great verse unto a little clan" which was *their* clan, so Klein writes as an intense individual out of one of those clans of which the texture of humanity is composed.

Poetry and the Jewish Tradition

Leon Edel

The following review article was part of a special Canadian number of Poetry, *Vol. LVIII (1941), pp. 51-53, copyright Leon Edel 1941. Reprinted by permission of the author.*

Leon Edel is the distinguished scholar and biographer of Henry James. An associate of the Montreal group, he has written at least three brief pieces on the work of Klein. The earliest was an essay in The Canadian Forum *(May, 1932) and the latest a review of* The Second Scroll *in* The Compass *(Sept. 23, 1951).*

The poetry of Abraham Moses Klein springs from the roots of a consciousness where Hebrew and legal lore have become strangely and exotically intermingled with Shakespeare and T. S. Eliot. Mr. Ludwig Lewisohn, in a preface to these verses, calls him "the first Jew to contribute authentic poetry to the literatures of English speech." Certainly Klein, heir to an authentic Jewish tradition, reflects that tradition in every line he writes. His verses are declamatory because far back the prophets too spoke as from the rooftops and because down the centuries Jews have, like Klein's Reb. Levi Yitschok, lectured to God. His wit is the dry wit of the mediaeval scholar; his reasoning is legalistic, not because he happens to be a lawyer, but because the talmudists were great reasoners and hair-splitters. His use of language is wholly Jewish in his search for high-sounding, pontifical words which, cunningly employed (as exemplified in Disraeli's classic reference to the gentleman

15

"intoxicated by the exuberance of his own verbosity") is exciting and exotic, but runs the risk of surfeiting the reader. One can almost hear Mr. Klein smacking his lips over

> Of yore yclept in old Judaea Zvi;
> Cognomen'd Cerf where Latin speech is carolled,
> Dubbed Hirsch, a transient, in wild Allmany,
> For sweet conformity now appellated Harold. . . .

A decade ago, when he was a young law student, he wrote of the "little Jew"—the junk dealer and the second-hand clothes man, the Jewish women at the market in Montreal's St. Lawrence Main, and brother Velvel, who nightly played cards in the back rooms of delicatessens and "garrulous barber shops," dreaming of the Rolls Royce he would like to own and the jewels for his wife

> . . . as large as wondrous eyes
> The eyes of Og, the giant king of Bashan.

These poems were close to the modern ghetto and therefore close to life; they were filled with witty observations and a delightful mixture of the real and the fantastic; they were pungent, vigorous and above all true.

Now he has collected a series of "Jewish" poems, built around quaint conceits and elaborate whimsicalities; poems of prayer for the fate of Israel, Chassidic dances, the legends and lore of the ghettoes of Prague and Warsaw. It is clear that the Hitlerian era of persecution has driven Klein far into the past. In his eloquent "Childe Harold's Pilgrimage," the beginning of which I have quoted, he comes to an ending of bland resignation:

> This only is mine wherewith to face the horde:
> The frozen patience waiting for its day,
> The stance long-suffering, the stoic word,
> The bright empirics that know well that the
> Night of the cauchemar comes and goes away,—

> A baleful wind, a baleful nebula, over
> A saecular imperturbability.

Klein is waiting for the Messiah.

"The stoic word" and the "bright empirics" make good reading, and entertaining reading; but one tires after a while of intellectual firecrackers and asks for a little more of the reality which A. M. Klein sees around him every day, as he must for instance, in the echoing corridors of the court house on Notre Dame Street east. In some of these poems an airy lyricism emerges, only to be smothered in euphuisms. The verse is always robust and there is much technical virtuosity; there is depth of feeling, as when he writes of Spinoza, and a lively sense of the incongruous. He tells pretty stories of kings and beggars—but they are all resigned beggars. The lack of discipline, which in his younger verse gave the sense of a rich vein of poetry flowing unchecked, now becomes a defect. There has been insufficient self-criticism. Lines such as

> He will go to the synagogue of Berditchev,
> And there sieve out his plaints in a dolorous sieve.

have been allowed to stand. One wishes that Klein had pressed a little harder.

The collection does Klein a distinct disservice in that it is not sufficiently representative of his remarkable gifts, the gift above all of eloquent rebellion. He quotes Shylock: "Hath not a Jew eyes? Hath not a Jew hands?" without Shylock's fierce defiance, closing his eyes and folding his hands and dreaming sweet dreams of a glamorous ghetto. He forgets that in Shylock there was no "frozen patience," for his passion and pride of race burned with a clear, angry, consuming flame.

And yet, despite their flaws, these poems are a poetic key to an ancient deep-rooted, emotional and intellectual tradition. As such they can lay claim to vitality and importance.

Review of *The Hitleriad*

E. J. Pratt

E. J. Pratt's review of The Hitleriad *appeared in* The Canadian Forum, *Vol. XXIV (1944), p. 164 and is reprinted by permission of the Estate of E. J. Pratt.*

Pratt had for some years been regarded as the leading Canadian poet. He appears to have liked The Hitleriad, *perhaps because it has some resemblance in technique and spirit to his own wartime poem "The Truant."*

Canadian poetry of recent years has been enriched by the work of A. M. Klein. He has not received the recognition in this country which he deserves although, we may be sure, his appearances in the United States through the New York publishing houses will help greatly to build up his audience here. For ten years or so discerning readers have felt the imaginative glow and peculiar power of his poems as they came out in the *Canadian Forum,* in *New Provinces,* and in *Hath Not A Jew.* He stood alone in his own classification, no other poet writing like him in Canada and, according to Ludwig Lewisohn, no one in the United States. His uniqueness consisted in his being the representative of Jewish nationalism, practically every important poem dealing with some phase of the tradition, religion, culture and outlook of the Hebrew race.

Such was the content and such the atmosphere enveloping it. But Klein also identified himself with a certain style which, though at first strikingly derivative of Eliot, brewed a tang of its own. It is true that a decade ago everybody was copying Eliot just as today so many of our new writers are being Spenderized into a family album. And when the "Soirée of Velvel Kleinberger" appeared, it was a little disconcerting to find that the voice of Velvel was that of Prufrock—"My life lies on a tray of cigarette butts." Still, Klein had a way of making us ignore the echoes by a manner of utterance which was imposed upon the material by the nature of the theme and by his own vivid personality. Despite the difficulties springing out of his scholasticism, his legalistic lore and his Talmudic terms and references which needed footnotes, Klein could appeal to us on the basis of a moral culture common to Jew and Gentile—that of the Hebrew prophet and psalmist. All of his best work possessed this appeal, whether it was the ringing affirmations of Isaiah or the subdued litanies of Jeremiah, Ecclesiastes and David. Moreover, he added something which can scarcely be attributed to the Old Testament—a rocket wit exploding in ironic contrasts and brilliant caricature.

The Hitleriad (published originally by *First Statement*) extends Klein's range both in material and treatment. It is written basically in the heroic couplet. In it he has discarded the musical instrument which played the lovely Biblical interludes of his Spinoza poem and such lyrics as Section vii:

> I am weak before the wind; before the sun
>   I faint; I lose my strength;
> I am utterly vanquished by a star,
>   I go to my knees, at length
> Before the song of a bird . . .

He has reverted to the more sinewy rhythms of his powerful "In Re Solomon Warshawer," although going beyond that war poem in fierceness of frontal assault. The pity and poignancy of "Warshawer" are displaced by militant blasts of denunciation and Drydenian satire. Indeed it is Dryden of Zimri and Achitophel, the politician, who is speaking in the lines. The satire is direct and unequivocal, leaving no room for any other interpretation than that of a face-to-face indictment, a bill of hate for the Nazi treatment of the Jew. Here is his picture of Hitler, the "artist":

> He drew a line, it was not crooked, so
> He thought that he was Michelangelo!
> Yet it is true that in due time, he would
> Incarnadine him murals with much blood;
> To Europe's marbled treasures adding his
> Ruins out-ruining Acropolis;
> Yes, with a continent for easel, he
> Would yet show vicious virtuosity,
> Would yet achieve the opus of his dream,
> The classic painting, masterpiece supreme:
> The Reich's *Last Supper* (out of stolen pots)
> With quislings six, and six iscariots!

There are no qualifications, no flanking innuendoes, nothing but the damnatory clauses pressed home to the hilt. Klein may be criticized here on academic grounds, that high satire, involving some reformative element, should not admit personal vituperation, but it is difficult to see how delicate, urbane shafts could be directed by a spokesman for the Ghetto against such targets as Hitler, Goering, Goebbels, Rosenberg, Ribbentrop and Ley. As well sharpen a rapier for a lunge at a Tiger tank. Klein must have anticipated this criticism in his invocation:

> Heil heavenly muse, since also thou must be
> Like my song's theme, a sieg-heiled deity,
> Be with me now, but not as once, for song:
> Not odes do I indite indicting Wrong!
> Be with me, for I fall from grace to sin,
> Spurning this day thy proferred hippocrene,
> To taste the poisoned lager of Berlin!

Klein has laid his plan of attack and has pursued it remorselessly. One may object to the stridency of some of the passages, to the punning, and to figures of speech which belong more to the vocabulary of oaths than of aesthetics, but few will deny the drive of the masculine thrust against the foes of humanity. No other poet today in this country has used the heroic couplet with greater pungency. The subject has pulled the threnodist away from the wall of lamentation and placed the satirist in a colosseum with a grenade in his hand and a good round curse on his lips.

Review of *The Hitleriad*

F. Cudworth Flint

This brief extract from a review of a number of new books of verse in The New York Times Book Review *(Sept. 3, 1944) is in interesting contrast to the remarks of E. J. Pratt.*

The Hitleriad tries to direct against Hitler the voice of public ridicule. But its author, Mr. Klein, has not enough ingenuity or verbal dexterity or malice—as distinguished from rage—to lead in such an enterprise. Most of his gibes are too laboured or else his tactics are inapposite. To write of Clemenceau as "The Tiger, ever-burning bright!" does not intensify the author's point; it merely frustrates the reader's emotions, because he feels that Blake's tiger and the French statesman, whatever his nickname, belong in disparate universes. I think also that a single verse-form maintained throughout the poem would, by the irony of its contrast with the muddled spasms of nazidom, have pointed the satire more than Mr. Klein's mixture of verse-forms.

Review of *Poems* (1944)

Irving Layton

Reprinted by permission of the authors from First State-ment, *Vol. II (1945), pp. 35-36.*

In this review Irving Layton develops further the criti-cism, first expressed in his review of The Hitleriad *(First Statement, Vol. II, No. 9, Oct.-Nov. 1944) of what he re-gards as Klein's failure to understand the nature of evil. Associated at this time with Louis Dudek and John Suther-land, he expresses, as they do, the attitudes of the newer "Montreal group" of the forties. Irving Layton is, in a sense, Klein's natural successor, as Leonard Cohen is his.*

Excepting the long, magnificent poem, "In Re War-shawer," the best of this volume lies in the 36 psalms in which A. M. Klein continues the passionate debate with the Deity he first began with the publication of *Hath Not A Jew.* The debate is of a high order; interesting because the principals are not without ability, humour, forceful eloquence, and repartee. God's repartee is the occasional thunder which breaks from his lips almost like a divine afterthought. Also His wisdom is darkly inscrutable and terrible — terrible because inscrutable. For sometimes through the cracks of His ineffable fingers He sends

> The fierce, carnivorous Messerschmidt,
> The Heinkel on the kill.

Or absent-mindedly employs

> . . . abominable scales
> on which the heavenly justice is mis-weighed.

The Lord, however, has been a member of the Jewish family for such a long time that disagreement with Him about His conduct is almost in the nature of a domestic quarrel. To the Jews He is an Elder Relative; in His more expansive moods the generous uncle, portly and a trifle deaf. To them He is neither a mystery nor the gaseous, elaborate construction of the metaphysicians. For this reason Klein's employment of the Absolute as a synonym for God has a quaint flavour about it; as though he were calling upon Him by a nickname.

To know God truly, one must have known Satan; Klein gives no evidence of ever having been within a hundred yards of that versatile gentleman. A brisk acquaintance with the latter might have injected a deeper note into some of the verses. As it is, the Psalms are not a record of spiritual trials undergone and the religious insights derived from them, so much as a recording of specific communicable emotions. Nonetheless, taken altogether, they wonderfully express the Jew's attitude toward his God, an attitude which is a rich and puzzling alloy of self-abasement and pride, of humility and defiance; it is one of accepting the heavenly scourge while establishing at the same time his human dignity by questioning necessity or its timing. It is this peculiarly intimate, sultry and difficult relationship between the Jews and their God which is revealed on almost every page of the Psalter. If the poems had no other virtues, this alone would make them memorable.

They have other virtues. The structure of these poems is simple, a fact that may warn off those who will not read a poem unless they're assured beforehand they won't understand it. The best of these poems have gusto, warmth, eloquence and imagination. They are as human as laughter is: Only a very few—Klein's weakness is a tendency towards rhetoric—are noisy and unconvincing. When he writes from a full passionate heart, out of pity and indignation, he is capable of such lines as

> They'll not be green for very long,
> Those pastures of my peace, nor will
> The heavens be a place for song,
> Nor the still waters still.

Abraham Moses Klein

A. J. M. Smith

This account of the evolving themes and techniques of Klein's work was published in a special issue of the Quebec periodical Gants du Ciel *(Printemps, 1946, pp. 67-81) and is reprinted by permission of the author.*

This and other articles were intended to introduce English-Canadian writers to a French-Canadian audience (a similar and hopefully more sustained effort of this kind is now under way in Ellipse, *a new magazine published at Sherbrooke University).*

A. J. M. Smith is well-known as a poet, critic and anthologist of distinction, and one of the original Montreal group. His essay may be contrasted with the very dim view of Klein's development that is expressed in the first article by John Sutherland. It was originally translated into French by Guy Sylvestre.

I

La poésie d'Abraham Moses Klein illustre admirablement le fait que les nouvelles tendances de la poésie, une expérimentation féconde et un modernisme progressif, sont le fruit de la maturité et de la sobriété et non de l'inexpérience et de l'enthousiasme incontrôlé. La poésie est un métier et un art à la fois, un effort commun en même temps qu'individuel, et ses traditions doivent être maîtrisées complètement avant de pouvoir être modifées ou portées plus loin. Si maintenant, dans ses plus récents poèmes qui ne sont pas encore recueillis en volume, M.

26

Klein se lance dans des expériences audacieuses et, la
plupart du temps, réussies, c'est qu'il a si complètement
assimilé la tradition poétique du dix-neuvième siècle dans
ses aspects humains et romantiques. Il est maintenant
capable, non en tournant le dos à la tradition mais en la
dépassant, d'aborder le présent immédiat et le lieu donné—
une rue juive, une ville cosmopolite, une province canadi-
enne-francaise.

Klein a publié trois volumes de vers—tous trois aux
Etats-Unis—*Hath Not a Jew* (1940), *The Hitleriad* (1944)
et *Poems* (1944). Quelques-uns de ses premiers poèmes
parurent dans la *McGill Fortnightly Review* et l'anthologie
canadienne *New Provinces,* tandis que ses oeuvres les plus
récentes ont été publiées dans le *Canadian Forum* et les
deux revues de Montréal *Preview* et *First Statement.* Bien
qu'il soit peut-être plus connu aux Etats-Unis que dans sa
patrie, M. Klein est de plus en plus reconnu, même ici,
comme le plus richement doué et le plus abondant de tous
les poètes canadiens de la génération postérieure à celle de
Pratt. Il a été judicieusement loué et intelligemment jugé
par deux des principaux critiques du Canada, W. E. Collin
dans *The White Savannahs* et E. K. Brown dans *On
Canadian Poetry.*

Il faut dire que la poésie de Klein nous est utile aujourd-
'hui parce qu'elle indique la valeur permanente d'une
tradition. Chez M. Klein, cette tradition est racial et
religieuse mais elle est aussi pratique et humaine, et cela
tempère l'humanisme intellectuel qui est un de ses carac-
tères par un humanitarisme intensément émotif, quoique
jamais sentimental. Nous devons nous demander dès le
début quelles sont les qualités de ce poète, comme homme
et comme artiste, qui déterminent ses sujets et condition-
nent son expression. Eh bien, ce sont une profondeur et
une intensité de sentiment, et ses sentiments les plus
intenses, ceux qu'il exprime avec le plus d'énergie et de
précision, sont les sentiments d'amour et de colère. Chez
lui la sympathie est agissante et énergique, et elle est la

source d'une ardeur lyrique qui donne un bonheur particulier à quelques-uns de ses poèmes les plus caractéristiques; et le sentiment opposé, celui de la colère ou de l'indignation, qui est aussi présent dans une grande partie de sa poésie, est mis en relief et parfois intensifié par l'ironie. Ces qualités, et les connaissances linguistiques et philosophiques qui ont rendu leur expression possible, peuvent être illustrées par quantité de ses meilleurs poèmes, mais il est important de signaler d'abord que ce qui éveille sa sympathie ou son indignation lui fait honneur comme homme et comme animal politique. Sa moralité est profonde, et il a l'humilité et la vénération d'un écrivain authentiquement religieux.

II

Examinons à la lumière de ces remarques deux des plus caractéristiques des premiers poèmes de Klein. Le plus impressionnant des poèmes élaborés de son premier volume porte le titre ironique "Childe Harold's Pilgrimage," et ce poème peut bien nous servir d'exemple de la poésie indignée et ironique que nous rencontrons si souvent dans les trois livres de Klein. Le pèlerinage en question est le voyage amer du Juif à travers l'histoire, de l'ancienne gloire à la présent destitution. Les premiers vers feront voir quelle maitrise Klein a de la technique, car le rythme et le style ont pour but d'y exprimer la dégradation progressive du héros symbolique.

> Of yore yclept in old Judaea Zvi;
> Cognomen'd Cerf where Latin speech is carolled;
> Dubbed Hirsch, a transient, in wild Allmany;
> For sweet conformity now appellated Harold,—
> Always and ever,
> Whether in caftan robed, or in tuxedo slicked,
> Whether of bearded chin, or of the jowls shaved blue,
> Always and ever have I been the Jew
> Bewildered, and a man who has been tricked. . . .

Remarquez l'archaïque grandeur rythmique du premier vers, l'ironique régression des verbes—"yclept," "cognomened," "dubbed,"—et la fadeur contemporaine des plats derniers vers. C'est grâce à ces ressources techniques et linguistiques subtiles que Klein atteint son but, qui est de souligner l'écart ironique entre la grandeur passée et la médiocrité présente et entre ce qui doit être et ce qui est. C'est le refus impérialiste au Juif d'un asile dans sa terre natale, qui engendre l'amertume dont le poème est plein:

> For they have all been shut, and barred, and triple-
>   locked,
> The gates of refuge, the asylum doors. . . .

A la vérité, il peut se rendre à la fascinante île de Madagascar

> Where in the sickly heat of noon I may
> Bloom, tropical, and rot, and happily melt away.

(Faut-il faire remarquer ici les riches ambiguïtés de l'accablant "happily"?) Ou encore, il peut être cordialement reçu en Russie—"Ay, but thy fell is somewhat safe in Muscovy!" Cela est admis comme une vérité, mais à quel prix, et un prix que Klein ne consentira jamais à payer—se défaire de ses "divine impedimenta" et laisser ses dieux lares à la douane. (Il faut de nouveau nous arrêter ici pour signaler la complexité ironique du ton et du sens du mot parfait et littéral "impedimenta".) Après avoir fait allusion avec une indignation méprisante à la Palestine sous mandat,

> Land of my fathers, cradle of my birth,
> Whither I may return, king to his throne,
> By showing the doorman Mr. Harold's worth
> Several thousand pounds (and not by loan!),

le poème examine le triste état des Juifs dans l'Allemagne hitlérienne. Un passage d'invectives enflammées qui an-

nonce la vigueur de son *Hitleriad* est suivi d'un acte
d'humilité dramatique et ironique:

> Is it my wealth you envy, my wine-goblet,
> My candlesticks, my spattered gaberdine?
> Why, take them; all my goods and chattels—yours.
> Take them, I shall not so much as say O,
> And let there be an end. The scowl persists.
> It is my thoughts, then, that you do begrudge me?
> Good; I'll expunge them! . . .

Le ton de ce passage, ceux qui se reporteront au poème le
verront, est une fusion réussie du poétique et du familier.
Dans sa gravité moqueusement sérieuse, cet air de condes-
cendance avec lequel on traite les enfants obstinés, est saisi
avec un habileté magistrale. Qu'est-ce qui vous ferait
plaisir? demande le protagoniste, qui ajoute:

> . . . Pray, do not tell me,
> I will find myself unfathom the dark reason.

Toute la situation est lestement sinistre et absurdement
enfantine. Le ton du poète indique qu'il reste au-dessous
de la vérité.

Mais le poème est plus qu'une attaque contre l'antisé-
mitisme nazi. Klein élargit la portée de sa critique ironique
en reconnaissant ce qui dans le monde chrétien a donné
aux nazis une arme si puissante:

> What is it, then,
> That ghostly thing that stalks between us, and
> Confounds our discourse? . . .
> I am too forward; wherever you seek me not
> There you do find me, always big in your sight.

Que cela soit déraisonnable et méchant, le ton seul l'impli-
que. Par contre, l'arme de Childe Harold est une soumis-
sion exagérée, une humilité également axagérée, quoique
ses ennemis soient trop peu sensibles pour apercevoir

l'ironie, sentir l'insulte ou reconnaître l'orgueil. Voici la suite:

> That, too, good brother, is no difficult matter—
> For I will dwarf myself and live in a hut . . .
> And speak so low that only God shall hear me!

Comment le poète résout-il le dilemme? Son père, nous dit-il,

> would don his prayershawl and pray.
> To him in converse with his God
> The wicked king was less than sod.

Mais Childe Harold ne peut trouver ainsi son salut. Il se décrit lui-même (nous ne devons pas oublier qu'il s'agit ici d'un poème de début. Je doute que M. Klein écrirait ce qui suit aujourd'hui.) comme

> . . . a pauper in spirit, a beggar in piety,
> Cut off without a penny's worth of faith.

Il ne peut non plus, en raison des commandements, recourir à la violence. Le suicide est rendu impossible par le respect de soi. Il ne rest que la résignation. À la fin, et à la fin seulement, le poème abandonne l'ironie consciente:

> This only is mine wherewith to face the horde:
> The frozen patience waiting for its day . . .
> Night of the cauchemar comes and goes away,
> A baleful wind, a baneful nebula, over
> A saecular imperturbability.

Seul le Juif, avec sa longue histoire de souffrance et de survivance, semble suggérer le poète, peut se permettre de telles paroles. Et pourtant, bien qu'il soit puissant par ses éléments négatifs de l'ironie et de la résignation, le poème ne nous satisfait pas entièrement. La raison en est, je crois,

que la foi et l'ardeur lyrique qui auraient pu rendre vic-
torieux son stoïcisme et son orgueil n'ont jamais pu s'exprimer dans ce poème. Klein a réservé ces sentiments pour
un autre poème, également ambitieux et plus impressionnant, une ode métaphysique et mystique inspirée par
Spinoza et intitulée "Out of the Pulver and the Polished
Lens."

La poème s'ouvre, il est vrai, sur une note d'ironie et de
courroux. Le poète dit son mépris de tous ces doctrinaires
pharisiens, juifs comme chrétiens, qui ont institutionalisé
Dieu. Le poète fuit la lettre qui tue et cherche avec
Spinoza un Dieu révélé par la passion intellectuelle. Il
trouve le secret de l'acceptation dans l'humilité et dans la
reconnaissance de la miraculeuse unité de l'individu et de
nature créé. La simplicité et la ferveur sont les caractéristiques du bref passage lyrique où cette foi est confessée:

> I am weak before the wind; before the sun
> I faint; I lose my strength;
> I am utterly vanquished by a star;
> I go to my knees, at length
>
> Before the song of a bird; before
> The breath of spring or fall
> I am lost; before these miracles
> I am nothing at all.

Cela nous conduit à la plus belle partie du poème, un
passage écrit dans la prose librement cadencée de la traduc-
tion anglaise des Psaumes. C'est un chant de déclaration
solennelle et de louange; là, "unto perfection a fragment
makes its prayer." Le mysticisme intellectuel de Spinoza
est présenté avec une ardeur lyrique qui est caractéristique
des meilleurs premiers poèmes de Klein. Les derniers vers
nous demandent de penser à Spinoza

> . . . gathering flowers for the One,
> the ever-unwedded lover of the Lord.

Je n'ai pas l'intention de signaler l'évolution de la pensée dans cet intéressant poème. J'en ai peut-être assez dit pour montrer que la source de l'orgueil religieux et racial de Klein se trouve dans son appréhension authentiquement spirituelle de l'unité de la nature créé par Dieu. Humilité devant les choses de Dieu, mais fierté devant les usurpations de l'homme: telles sont les attitudes que ce poète de la moderne Judée exprime dans tous ses poèmes, parfois unies comme dans le beau poème de guerre qui est peut-être la plus belle pièce des *Poems* (1944), la rhapsodie dramatique inspirée par la tragédie du ghetto de Varsovie et intitulée "In re Solomon Warshawer."

Ici Childe Harold est devenu digne et d'une stature tragique. Dans la personne du vieux Juif en haillons, le voyageur exilé, le véritable roi Salomon de la religion antique détrôné par le Malin, l'usurpateur Asmodée, Salomon Warshawer condamne le fol usurpateur du monde moderne, Hitler, et il ne parle pas seulement au nom du poète ou de la seule race juive, mais au nom de toute l'humanité dont la dignité et l'inviolabilité sont profanées par la cruauté ou l'oppression. Ce courroux, cette fierté, cet héroisme sont d'order politique. Le Juif opprimé se tourne vers ses bourreaux nazis et leur crie son mépris:

> The dwarf dictators, the diminutive dukes,
> The heads of straw, the hearts of gall,
> Th' imperial plumes of eagles covering rooks!

Passant en revue la longue histoire des empires qui l'ont persécuté, son orgueil a la dureté et la concision classiques:

> And now, albeit I walk raggedly,
> I walk; and they are echoes to my tread!

Mais l'orgueil et l'amertume sont anéantis dans l'affirmation extatique de la dignité divine de l'homme, et c'est cette attitude et son expression dans le poème qui donnent à cette oeuvre son sens universel. Solomon Warshawer n'est pas le Juif éternel; il est l'Homme, l'enfant de la nature et le fils de Dieu:

> Is there great turmoil in the sparrow's nest
> When that bright bird, the Sun, descends the west?
> There is no fear, there is no twittering;
> At dawn they will again behold his brightly plumaged
>   wing!
> Such is the very pattern of the world,
> Even the sparrows understand;
> And in that scheme of things am I enfurled. . . .
>
> Mistake me not: I am no virtuous saint;
> Only a man, and like all men, not godly,
> Damned by desire—
> But I at least waged war, for holy booty,
> Against my human taint;
> At least sought wisdom, to discern the good;
> Whether of men, or birds, or beasts of the wood;
> Spread song, spread justice; ever did aspire—
> Howbeit, man among men, I failed—
> To lay the plan, and work upon the plan
> To build the temple of the more-than-man!

Ce n'est pas là la poésie d'un Chrétien et d'un Catholique, mais ce la pourrait être. C'est, d'après Mr. Ludwig Lewisohn, la poésie "du plus juif des poètes qui s'expriment en anglais," la poésie d'un avocat de Montréal.

III

Klein est un poète très humain. Il sait que l'homme ne peut vivre dans la solitude. Il est par conséquent un poète de la société et de la famille. L'amour d'une société sévère et patriarcale avec ses cérémonies et ses mythes lui est congénital. Grâce à l'assurance et à la certitude de comprendre qu'un tel sens de l'interdépendance peut donner, Klein a créé une poésie familière, simple et «paroissiale».

Plusieurs de ses brefs poèmes lyriques ont un charme particulier qui leur vient de la légèreté et de la grâce de sa
fantaisie, de la tendresse et de la subtilité de son humour.
Certains d'entre eux, comme "A Deed of Daring" ("How
Samson got the rabbi a herring") ou "Cantor"

> With portly belly
> A cantor comes
> Through musical nostrils
> He sweetly hums—

sont d'un fort comique; d'autres, comme "Baal Shem Tov"
(le saint François juif), le délicieux "Bestiary," ou le pro-
fondément sensible "Heirloom," avec son apogée soudain
et intense, unissent l'humour à une violence qui est relevée
par la grâce lyrique.

Toutes ces qualités peuvent être vérifies dans un important poème récent qui, bien qu'il ne se trouve pas dans
les *Poems,* est reproduit dans *The Book of Canadian
Poetry.* En écrivant le plus personnel de ses poèmes, Mr.
Klein semble avoir tiré profit de l'exemple de W. B. Yeats,
dont les derniers poèmes-souvenirs, mi-familiers, mi-exaltés,
sont un modèle que le poète a su imiter sans toujours
tomber dans la servilité. La forme de la strophe, les passage
parfaitement effectué du style familier au style noble, et
les subtiles modulations du rythme, tout indique le talent
avec lequel Klein a su se mettre à l'école du maître. Le
poème débute par une saisissante évocation du quartier
juif de Montréal vu avec l'ardeur propre aux souvenirs
d'enfance:

> Out of the jargoning city I regret
> Rise memories, like sparrows rising from
> The gutter-scattered oats—

souvenirs de la boulangerie, du salon de barbier, et par-
dessus tout de la sombre synagogue et de son brouhaha
religieux. Ces lieux lui rappellent ses soeurs, son frère

aîné et les gaies excursions d'été à la ferme, ainsi que la
réception chez lui de deux étrangers qui venaient d'échap-
per à un massacre polonais:

> The cards and humming stop.
> And I too swear revenge for that pogrom.

Le souvenir de ses parents est mêlé de souvenirs de cérémonies et d'histoires religieuses, comme sa mère portant
une perruque varsovienne et bénissant les cierges sacrés
ou son père portant le petit garçon au lit—

> O memory of unsurpassing love,
> Love leading a brave child
> Through childhood's ogred corridors, unfear'd!

La poète se souvient aussi des jeux d'enfance dans les rues
de la ville, et l'intensité du poète augmente ensuite dans
les deux dernières strophes, dont je ne citerai que la
première:

> Immortal days of the picture-calendar
> Dear to me always with the virgin joy
> Of the first flowing of the senses five
> Discovering birds, or textures, or a star,
> Or tastes, sweet, sour, acid, those that cloy,
> And perfumes. Never was I more alive.
> All days thereafter are a dying-off,
> A wandering away
> From home and the familiar. The years doff
> Their innocence.
> No other day is ever like that day.

IV

Depuis deux ou trois ans, la technique et l'inspiration de
Klein ont changé. Seule l'attitude fondamentale, l'humanité et la sympathie, est restée la même. Stimulé en

partie par ses relations avec les poètes plus jeunes du groupe de *Preview,* particulièrement, semblerait-il, P. K. Page et Patrick Anderson, il a construit quelques-uns de ses plus récents poèmes à l'aide d'une série d'images spirituelles ou de concepts métaphysiques. Il s'est livré à des expériences de télescopage joycien de mots ou de syllabes, et a permis à son érudition linguistique et philosophique de se manifester d'une manière à la fois amusante et intensément grave. Mais, ce qui est plus important, il a substitué au monde juif un autre monde, qui n'est pas sans analogies avec le premier. Ces poèmes sont les premiers essais d'une interprétation de la province de Québec en regard desquels ceux de tout autre écrivain anglais semblent fades et faibles. Dans l'entité patriarchale, traditionnelle et ecclésiastique qu'est le Canada français, Klein a trouvé un univers que sa sensibilité juive lui permet de comprendre et d'aimer. Voici un peuple heureux qu'il ne peut s'empêcher d'envier, une tribu fortement enracinée dans les traditions ancestrales, unie, surveillée par une caste d'ecclésiastiques, garantie par ses propres lois, sa langue propre, possédant sa terre à lui, priant dans ses propres églises et libre de diriger sa destinée. Il peut compendre ses aspirations parce qu'elles sont celles de son propre peuple, bien que les Canadiens soient en sûreté chez eux alors que les siens sont dispersés et opprimés.

Ainsi, dans un de ses plus récents poèmes, il dit de la berceuse d l'habitant:

It seconds the cricket of the province. Heard
in the clean lamplit farmhouses of Quebec,
wooden, it is no less a national bird;
and rivals, in its cage, the mere stuttering clock.
To its time, the evenings are rolled away;
and in its peace the pensive mother knits
contentment to be worn by her family,
grown-up, but still cradled by the chair in which she sits.

. . . .

It rolls with the gait of St. Malo. It is act

and symbol, symbol of this static folk
which moves in segments, and returns to base—
a sunken pendulum: *invoke, revoke*;
loosed yon, leashed hither, motion on no space.
Oh, like some Anjou ballad, all refrain,
which turns about its longing, and seems to move
to make a pleasure out of repeated pain,
its music moves, as if always back to a first love.

Ou encore, dans les "Snowshoers," il découvre dans la
paysage hivernal de Québec le sujet de ce qui est sans
contredit un des poèmes les plus gais et les plus charmants
qu'un Canadien ait jamais écrits. Les couleurs, la glace,
les attitudes et le mouvements font singulièrement songer
à un Kreighof. Le lecteur m'excusera de citer encore.
Voici les première et troisième strophes de ce poème.:

The jolly icicles ringing in their throats,
their mouths meerschaums of vapour,
from the saints' parishes they come, like snowmen
spangled, with spectrum colour
patching the scarf green, sash red, sky-blue the coat—
come to the crystal source. Their airy hooves
Unslung from their backs are ready
to stamp their goodlucks on the solid foam. . . .
O gala garb, bright with assomption . . .
A candy-coloured world!
And moods as primary as their tuques and togs—
of tingling cold, and the air rubbed down with snow
and winter well-being! . . .

And now, clomping the packed-down snow of the street
they walk on sinews
gingerly, as if their feet were really swollen,
eager for release
from the blinders of buildings; suddenly they cut
a corner, and—the water they will walk!
Surf of the sun!

World of white wealth! Wind's tilth! Waves
of dazzling dominion
on which their coloured sails will billow and rock!

Qui peut s'empêcher de s'écrier: Quelle gaîté! quel ardent
amour de la vie! Quelle clarté et innocence du regard!
Mais il ne faut pas oublier de remarquer l'habileté et la
science si facilement dissimulées: songez à la richesse de
sens et de suggestion des mots «assomption» et «dominion»
tels qu'ils sont employés ici.

D'autres poèmes qui sont de la même manière comprenn-
ent le poème bilingue "Montreal"—inégal, me semble-t-il,
et le grave et brillant hymne au pain: "Bread." Ces poèmes
sont d'audacieuses expériences par leur imagerie, leur
rythme et leur style, mais ils possèdent en commun un
élément qui est plus important que leur technique, et c'est
leur ton, l'attitude, le point de vue qu'ils trahissent. Tous
—et cela est conforme au développement de l'art de Klein—
énoncent des vérités simples, les grandes vérités de la vie.
Ils sont traditionnels, essentiellement conservateurs, et fon-
damentalement classiques. Humanité, ordre, joie et foi
sont les mots-clefs de cette poésie. Klein les a découverts
dans l'orthodoxie juive et il commence à les découvrir dans
une race qui n'a pas toujours manifesté beaucoup de sympathie pour la sienne.

La gravité du rôle du poète, sa place dans la société, et
la nécessité d'une incessante quête de nouveaux modes de
connaissance et d'expression: tels sont les thèmes du
dernier et du plus long des récents poèmes de Klein, le
"Portrait of the Poet as a Nobody," publié l'été dernier
dans *First Statement*. Les derniers vers peuvent être con-
sidérés comme le testament du plus brillant et du plus
sérieux des poètes canadiens-anglais:

To find a new function for the declassé craft
archaic like the fletcher's; to make a new thing;

to say the word that will become sixth sense;
perhaps by necessity and indirection bring
new forms to life, anonymously, new creeds—
O, somehow pay back the daily larcenies of the lung!

These are not mean ambitions. It is already something
merely to entertain them. Meanwhile, he
makes of his status as zero a rich garland,
a halo of his anonymity,
and lives alone, and in his secret shines. . . .

The Poetry of A. M. Klein

John Sutherland

John Sutherland's essay on Klein appeared in Index *(Aug. 1946, pp. 8-12, 20-21) and is reprinted here by permission of the Estate of John Sutherland.*

This is the first very stringent criticism that Klein received. John Sutherland was the founder and editor of First Statement, *whose most notable contributors were Irving Layton, Louis Dudek, Miriam Waddington and Raymond Souster. These poets aimed at a purer and simpler language, at the local and particular, and rejected the cosmopolitanism and "metaphysical" style of Smith, Klein, Patrick Anderson, P. K. Page and the other poets associated with the rival magazine* Preview. *Sutherland moved eventually from a realist to a Catholic position. This can be seen in his last publication* The Poetry of E. J. Pratt *(1956).*

"Autobiographical" is one of the best of recent poems by A. M. Klein, and one of the most significant for understanding the poet's development since the early *Hath Not A Jew*. Klein—who was hailed by the sentimental Lewisohn as the potentially great "poet of a clan"—has moved so far from his early work that he is rarely even writing on Jewish themes. "Autobiographical" is a record of the people the poet knew as a boy, of the city he was brought up in, and of the fossilized attitudes which helped to

41

produce *Hath Not A Jew*. "I am no old man", he tells us, "fatuously intent on memoirs, but

> . . . in memory I seek
> The strength and vividness of nonage days,
> Not tranquil recollection of event.
> It is a fabled city that I seek,
> It stands in space's vapours and time's haze.

The fabled city of childhood—of a great people and their romantic past, so much alive for the boy and the young man, is now something to be sought after through memory "productive of the sadness of remembered joy." When Klein talks of "the ghetto streets where a Jewboy/Dreamed pavement into pleasant Bible-land," he uses the past tense, and consciously or not, writes an epitaph for his early poetry. "Autobiographical" describes the space and time location, the actual setting in which *Hath Not A Jew* was produced. The real scene has displaced the fabled city, as the power to describe it has triumphed over the knack of transforming it into a romantic dream. The past is in process of being understood, but its strength and vividness are disappearing at the same time.

The critics of *Hath Not A Jew* adopted far too solemn a tone. The introduction by Lewisohn, the book's title, the "Childe Harold's Pilgrimage" and other serious poems at the beginning of the volume—these were all taken by the critics at face value when they were only so much camouflage. As a disciplinary measure, they should be required to read *Hath Not A Jew* again, beginning with the poems on children at the end of the book and reading backwards till they get their perspective straight. They would discover that the child was the "Leader" for whom the string music was written; that the "little hunter" trailing "the beast Nebuchadnezzar" was a miniature replica of the rabbi "splitting/hairs"; that the fairy tales in verse differed only in degree from the previous descriptions of the Jews' age-long sufferings; that the scholarly goat, the "Venerable Bee," the "Rev. Owl," were brothers under the skin to Reb Simcha, Solomon Talmudi, and the other worthies portrayed elsewhere. The themes of the adult section are different from those of the children section, but the similarity of mood and tone makes this unimportant. The more we read *Hath Not A Jew* the more we realize that the real world is made an excuse for escaping into a world of romance, and that people and their tragedies are dissolved by the childlike fancy playing over them. Of course, there are poems in the book which do not re-create but falsify reality. I feel that the bulk of the love poems, like the philosophic poems, distort things in the interest of a sentiment or prejudice, and that Klein is not the poet to express a serious idea or even a serious emotion. But when he captures one facet of a character or situation, and transforms it with the colours of his fancy, he produces genuine poetry. The caricature of Moses, "Elijah," the landlord, the marriage broker and others are the best things in *Hath Not A Jew*, and infinitely superior to the solemn pieces the critics have admired.

Klein's art of caricature is like the popular game of pinning the tail on the donkey. The donkey subject—a strip of plain cloth—can be safely ignored in favour of the tail which is being pinned on him. Better if one goes at him blind, because then there is no bar to one's fancy and no end to the surprising things that can happen. Better too if there are a number of failures or near-misses, because the whole fun lies in the cumulative efforts to put the tail on straight. Klein has almost literally made his junk-dealer a donkey in the stanza

> While litanies are clamoured,
>   His loud voice brags.
> A Hebrew most ungrammared
>   He sells God rags.

But less obviously he has done the same thing with all his characters. His landlord is shorn of all dignity:

> He is a learned man, adept
>   At softening the rigid.
> Purblind, he scans the *rashi* script,
>   His very nose is digit.

Elijah, trying to amuse the children, is a delightful idiot:

> He crows like a rooster,
> He dances like a bear,
> While the long-faced rabbis
> Drop their jaws to stare.

In these abbreviated sketches, in which Klein gets hold of one facet of a character and runs it to the ragged limit, the persons portrayed suffer loss of dignity and come through the grilling something less than men. *Hath Not A Jew* is the portrait of a fascinating zoo, rather than a human community; it is like a series of comic illustrations for a book of nursery rhymes. Klein, having sat at the feet of Elijahs, who could tell "tall tales about the Baal Shem Tov," learned to repeat the stories with more humour and greater imagination. With his first book he returned, not to those he "roistered with in his salad days," but to the remarkable people who shared in his eyes, the glamour of the kings and heroes they described to him. Who could say that the book is not the product of an enthusiastic admiration for Elijah:

> Between the benedictions
> We would play leap-frog—
> Oh this was a wonderful
> Synagogue.

"Benediction and leap-frog" is a fair description of these alternately pious and impious early poems.

Of course, the book was conceived in a more serious light and even the skilful caricatures are affected by its philosophy. In "Sophist" there is a scepticism reminiscent of Eliot:

> The skull replete with pilpul tricks
> Has long returned to its matrix,
> Where worms split hair, where Death confutes
> The hope the all-too-hopeful moots.

But Klein has less in common with Eliot than with a nineteenth-century writer like Fitzgerald, the translator of the Rubaiyat of Omar Khayyam. Reading the "Talisman in Seven Shreds" one is reminded of the Rubaiyat in lines like

> Do you your genuflexions to the Rose,
> Be merry, eat and drink, the large paunch crows

or in

> To sleep, perchance to dream.
>   Where there is smoke
> There is fire. Death does not end the act.

Although the poet is not satisfied with his model, and in a sense is rejecting it ("Be it the spirit or the dust I hoe/ Only at doomsday's sunrise will I know") he seems to find the romantically cheerful scepticism of the Rubaiyat very much to his taste. He could not accept the attitude of the early Eliot without shattering the dream world of *Hath Not A Jew*; but the exotic philosophy of the Fitzgerald poem, offering so much consolation and such latitude of belief, is suited to the balance of scepticism and sentimentality on which the book depends. Death "confutes" the Sophist only until he arrives in heaven:

> But I think that in Paradise
> Reb Simcha with his twinkling eyes,
> Interprets in some song-spared nook
> To God the meaning of his book.

And this stanza, following hard on the heels of the Death stanza, carries us from despair to the heights of heaven in a single swoop. Elijah may look very ridiculous "crowing like a rooster," but he is also a bit of a miracle man:

> Wished he, he could gather
> The stars from the skies,
> And juggle them like marbles
> Before our very eyes.

No situation is so grim that it does not offer an outlet for the largest hope. A man may be a fool, and somewhat less than a man, but that does not prevent him from being divine. Or, to put it another way—and here we touch on something essential both to the poetry and the philosophy —the great is very small, but what is small knows no limitations. The great is small—whatever is abstract must be made concrete, whatever is big and difficult must become minute and trivial. The shock of the wit lies in the contrast of dimensions that do not agree. God is given a human form and is left alone "twiddling his contented thumbs"; man is reduced to a little dust that shifts over to make room for more dust. Eventually we arrive at the "slimy exegetes" who "mark exegesis upon the parchment-browed"; but having arrived there we are only at the beginning of our travels. Have we descended the long ladder that joins the grave and heaven, going all the way from the top to the very bottom? Then what is to stop us, standing here on the lowest rung of the ladder, from proceeding to climb back again? As long as one slimy exegete shall be saved, the disaster of scepticism can be transformed into the success of belief. What Klein says of Spinoza is also true, in his own way, of Klein: "From glass and dust he brought to light—the prism and the flying mote; and hence the infinitesimal and infinite—. Even on the numb legs of a snail thou dost move O Lord. A babe in swaddling clothes laughs at the sunbeams on the door's lintel; the sucklings play with thee. . . ." Abraham and

Simchka can say with Spinoza: "I behold thee in all things: Lo, it is myself; I look into the pupil of thine eye, it is my eye." So that, if the rabbis look very much like donkeys, remember that the donkey is also made in the image of the Lord. It is a fair question whether or not the donkey *is* the Lord. Does he perhaps create him in order to have a mirror for his virtue?

Insofar as *Hath Not A Jew* is what the title suggests— an ironic argument that the Jew is also a human being— I feel it falls short of being convincing. Klein's plea that we are "all human beings," and that therefore we should understand each other and be able to live in harmony has been made unsuccessfully so many times that we are bound to be sceptical of it. While the ghetto and the world remain unchanged, goodwill must create a revolution which the nature of things stubbornly resists. Isn't this idea part of the romance of *Hath Not A Jew*; isn't it born of the situation it deplores? The ideal human being in whose name Klein speaks, was never born of woman and bears no relation to any person who has lived; he "issues, as from a chrysalis, from the God of the mono- theistic religions." Klein ensures this god his immortality, and by keeping the figurehead intact with the vessel, guarantees the continued hostility of Jew and Gentile. He will speak of religion as an "old fraud," and of himself as "cut off without a penny's worth of faith," but he cannot see the relation of the old fraud to the old system, and never searches far enough to discover the cause of the trouble. He upholds a sentimental ideal of tolerance, fail- ing to realize that the historical role of tolerance has been to accumulate oppression.

If this flabbiness of thought mattered little in *Hath Not A Jew,* where the ideas are rightly subordinate to the fancy, we will find it of prime concern in Klein's later poetry. *Hath Not A Jew,* published in 1940, was followed in 1944 by *The Hitleriad,* and in the same year by *Poems,* a volume of "psalms." *Poems* may seem of little impor-

tance, containing, as it does, earlier work which might
have been published in *Hath Not A Jew* but which was
probably better left out. Klein, affirming his faith (see
Psalm 2), and asking for guidance from above, is not very
convincing and certainly very dull. However, a number of
poems, reflecting the growth of fascism and the coming of
war, point in the direction which Klein's poetry took with
the publication of *The Hitleriad*. In this long satire on the
Nazis and Naziism, Klein is identifying himself with the
Jewish prophets:

> I am the grandson of the prophets! I
> Shall not seal lips against iniquity,
> Let anger take me in its grasp; let hate,
> Hatred of evil prompt me, and dictate!

As grandson of the prophets, Klein is adopting an
entirely new role. It wasn't the prophets but the eating
and drinking Reb Abrahams who fascinated him in his
early poems. The skinny "mortifiers of the flesh"—those
who were sick and moral at the same time—were only considered by special favour and were never given differential
treatment. Now Klein refuses to seal lips against iniquity,
declares furiously against it, and is at the same time
humble in his certainty that God "will rise, will shine,
will stretch forth his right hand/And strike them down."
Again it does not matter whether "the Lord of Hosts" is
to be taken seriously or is only a piece of literary fur-
niture. What does matter is that Klein is riding the moral
hobby-horse and that he is there to stay. Bad and good are
as different as black is from white. All the vices and evil
forces are so tangible, so readily ascertainable, that they
can be capitalized and personified as they are in ancient
scripts; all the virtues and good powers are made to go
through the same transmogrification. Evil is the evil of the
melodrama, and is expressed in melodramatic terms like
"the grim vulture of the brood/Its talons dripping blood";
the good is melodramatic good, and its success is belated

and inexplicable, but inevitable and final. So Klein blithely avers "And on that day as the unrighteous pass/ Unrighteousness will pass away," goes on to describe "the fields glowing with argosies," and further declares that:

> Man will don his godliness once more . . . .
> Man loyal to the human brotherhood,
> To human brotherhood, and to the godly reign.

To that godhood which, as we saw in *Hath Not A Jew*, comprised Ideal Man and the Lord of Hosts, Virtue is now added and the trinity become complete. Are there any weak points in this three-headed faith? Is Man or is Virtue unreal? Is the Lord of Hosts unreal? We should be very cautious, because this chain is no stronger than any of its links.

Just what Klein does believe, however, is not so definite as this suggests; and when we consider his other new poems we see how varied and contradictory his opinions can be. "In Memoriam," far from assuming man's essential goodness and the triumph of virtue, would have us believe that man was irrevocably bad and that vice was omnipresent and permanent. "Pawnshop" shows the human race in pawn without so much as a pawn ticket to buy its way out. Kleinian philosophy is just as much at the mercy of Kleinian wit as it was in *Hath Not A Jew*, but now Klein is ready to utter even a contradiction dogmatically. If we attempted to sum up the change, we would simply say: Dogmatism has killed the poetry. In *The Hitleriad*, the white hope Dogmatism disposed of the black killer in a rousing battle, but also felled the referee with an axe-like blow. To get on with the simile, the referee was poetry—the referee tried to stand in the gap and stop the wholesale slaughter, and got killed in the process. *The Hitleriad* is to be judged as most people judge a boxing fight—does it or does it not make you fighting mad? The best passages in the poem—the slangy portraits of Goebbels, Goering, Ribbentrop and others—are unconditional

surrender pieces, giving no quarter to their opponents.
Art is made identical with abuse. *The Hitleriad* is a
polemic, and a polemic that might have achieved its purpose as well in prose as in metres. Certainly if we look in
it for the suggestibility of poetry, or the subtle wisdom of
satire, we are doomed to disappointment.

If we examine *The Hitleriad* more carefully we see that
it was conceived as a poetic trial of Hitler and Naziism,
and that Klein cast himself not so much in the role of
prophet as of prosecuting attorney. He has given us the
clue with his pun in line 4—"Not odes do I indite, indict-
ing Wrong"—and also significant is the demonstrative presentation of evidence ("And let the world see that swastika
stain"). He begs the Muse:

> Aid me, and in good time, for as I talk
> The knave goes one step nearer to the dock.

He demands that the reader "See him, the culprit twelve
men damn," and asks for "the dossier, the facts, the untam-
pered texts." Had Hitler been caught and hanged, Klein's
poem might have achieved a great notoriety, for the lines
just quoted are not merely poetic conceits but indicate that
the poetic method has a legal twist. The first two-thirds of
the poem are devoted to an elaborate and detailed presentation of the "evidence." Hitler's "vegetarian blob" of a
face, Goebbel's halitosis, Goering's "tub" of a stomach, and
Ribbentrop's Bond Street sophistication are exhibited to
judge and jury along with a documentation of Nazi crimes
attested to by the witnesses "from wagons sealed in a forgotten land." Finally, the initial stages of the trial give way
to a summation of evidence and an impassioned appeal to
the jury:

> Thief, perjurer, blasphemer, murderer,
> Let him be blotted out, and all his crew.
> Efface the evil; let it be no more.
> Let the abomination cease; and through
> Implacable justice let emerge the world clean, new!

A pattern was established that would be followed in later poems.

All the recent works are half poetic and half legalistic. Legal metaphors infest them, and a number of them are conceived in the form of a trial (compare "In Memoriam" and "In Re Solomon Warshawer"). Directly or indirectly they all follow the pattern of presentation of the evidence first and summation to the jury afterwards. Up to the last stanza Klein is busy collecting and presenting the numbered exhibits—the whole sum of little details and odd facts drawn directly from experience. Thus he offers in "Pawnshop":

> The dear, the engraved, the boasted inventory;
> The family plate hocked for the widow's mite;
> The birthday gifts; the cups of victory;
> The unpensioned tools; the vase picked up in Crete;
> The hero's medal; ring, endowing bride;
> Camera; watch; lens; crushed accordion,

and so on ad infinitum. We may note that most of these details are bare and uninteresting in themselves; that they tend to repeat and turn back on one another; and that ultimately they kill, rather than accelerate, the poem's progress. We are bothered because we are aware that each of them has been selected with an almost mathematical care. Each word, and even each syllable is studied so long that we feel as if the poem were being slowly pulverized before our eyes, ground up into dust and little particles which refuse to cohere. All of Klein's recent poems are, in the initial stages, catalogues rather than compositions. And when we come to the final stanza—the whopping generalization, the summation to the jury—

> All
> are carnivrous. Almost all men's meat is cannibal.
> Invoking a great word like you we strive;
> like you we prosper only on defeat—

it is just as if Klein approached something which was
undoubtedly dead and tried to revive it with artificial
respiration. If a poem needs to be tagged with a general
conclusion, then surely that is proof that something is
wrong with it. The general idea should suggest itself
through the details of the poem, and not require a pains-
taking and exact expression. We go to such lengths to con-
struct an edifice—and then what do we discover? That we
forgot about the corner-stone and must now set it up on
top of the whole pile. Moreover, while we are firmly convinced of the existence of the corner-stone, and of the
necessity for it, we seem to believe that any corner-stone
will do for any building. At bottom we regard it as a kind
of architectural flourish, which may have meaning or may
not, but which shall convince the spectator that the construction has no flaw. One conclusion at one time, and
another at another time—but would it matter so much if
we exchanged the conclusions?

Technically too Klein has changed radically, and
changed, I feel, for the worse. The abbreviated stanzas of
Hath Not A Jew, with their frequent feminine endings,
their sudden and unexpected movements, have slowed
down into a funeral procession of iambic pentameters, cal-
culated geometrics, and ponderous stanzas that seem carved
from stone. The archaic phrasing which added a fillip to
the rhythms of *Hath Not A Jew*, has become the pedantry
of incessant inversion and qualification:

> Myself was not more kindliness; I deemed
> You—thought unspoken—of a hell of a breed,
> as man miscarried; charming, if a snake.
> You python knowledge gleamed
> With clues, crimes, and not-guiltys always faked.

"Myself was not"; "I deemed"; "thought unspoken"—such
phrases indicate a belief that rhetoric can be passed off as
poetry. "You python knowledge gleamed" may not imme-

diately make sense, but the inversion was necessary to get a
rhyme for "deemed." These lines are followed by the catalogue of a conversation:

> You talk of hanged men, shocked, expelling seed—
> O love and Death upon the frightening stage!—
> of trite confession, last gastronomy,
> of the men docile, of those loud with rage,
> all curiosa of the fatal tree,
> the bitter apples of your pilgrimage,
> tempted; and, now I say it, jaundiced me.

We are faced here with similar difficulties: first that of
unwinding the inward syntax of the "Love and Death"
line, and getting out of the blind alley of the successive
parallels to discover the main verb "tempted," then that
of a rhetoric which relies for its force upon abstractions
like Love and Death, on clichés like "loud with rage,"
and on repetition with pedantic variation as in the third
and second last lines. We cannot avoid concluding that the
bulk of Klein's later work in spite of many witty passages
and better poems like "Caughnawauga" and "Portrait of
the Poet as a Nobody" is an example of padding or involvement as an excuse for very little or nothing to say. As the
short rhymed stanza of *Hath Not A Jew* was suitable to
the light and mocking tone of the poetry—to its essentially
trivial but delightful substance—so the stanza, at once
roomy and complicated of these later poems, is tailored to
the need of an over-meticulous and platitudinous thought-
process. In the second case, consistency seems fatal.

Klein, of course, has attempted to foster this development. Disillusioned with "the solitaire of rhyme and wit"
when he came to write *The Hitleriad*, he felt the need of
acquiring philosophic girth and of dealing with more
serious subjects on a larger scale. His new intellectuality is
intended as a bow to modern poetry, as are his changes
in technique. His slower and more colloquial rhythms,
with their inwoven and partly disguised rhyme, should be

contrasted with the musical lilt of *Hath Not A Jew* and *Poems*. He was able to give an impression of modernity because of the continued deference of the modern school to the eighteenth century, and because his urban and didactic poetry, is in fact, a minor descendant of the satire of Pope and Dryden. But that Klein can be "modern" in appearance only, and that his relationships to the eighteenth century is on the imitative rather than the creative level, seems to me evident from a study of his poetry. The poems in *Hath Not A Jew*, particularly the caricatures in words, remain the superior achievement and are likely to be read in Canada long after the weightier works are forgotten.

Review of *The Rocking Chair*

Margaret Avison

This review appeared in The Canadian Forum, *Vol. XXVIII (1948), p. 191, and is reprinted by permission of the author.*

Margaret Avison is probably Canada's most important female poet. Her two books are Winter Sun *and* The Dumbfounding. *Her work is very difficult and intricate, but it is possible to speculate that her appreciation of Klein's new technical directions in* The Rocking Chair *influenced her. At the very least, the two poets share a few "Canadian" concerns, e.g. the problem of space and landscape, the concern for perception as creation (as in "Portrait of the Poet as Landscape"), the issue of perspective.*

When a complete collection of the poetry of A. M. Klein is published, it should include several facsimiles of his manuscripts. Freakish and irrelevant as the notion may sound, one cannot help feeling that some of Mr. Klein's artistry is lost when his own drawing of letters and words is lost. All poetry gives words multiple meaning: literal, associative, mimetic, musical. But Mr. Klein's poetry gives one a startled feeling about the letters that make up the words. Fleetingly, again and again, individual letters emerge with their own absolute meanings which are submerged within the words' sense but independent both of this and of the technical function of the particular vowel or consonant in its context. An eery feeling of buried wit is the result particularly in "Winter Night: Mount Royal," and it becomes charmingly explicit on the very next page

55

in the line "the horsemen on their horses like the tops of f's."

The precision of Mr. Klein's writing recalls Rubens' painting of lace collars and embroidered vestments, for very rarely does the detail distract one from a poem's total meaning. Like Demosthenes, Mr. Klein knows that everybody's speech is defective, and he has in his humility accepted Demosthenes' corrective pebbles. There are phrases here and there where the pebbles are just a mouthful, for example the "poised for parabolas" in the very beautiful poem "Lone Bather." But one almost welcomes these bad moments, because they clearly establish what is wrong with a number of apprentice poets who have learned to mouth the pebbles without realizing what Mr. Klein knows so well—that their whole purpose is to discipline speech into clarity. Every poem in this collection is built on the iambic pentameter line, although almost every line is a variant of this rhythm, and the quiet shuttling in and out of rhyme and half-rhyme marks still further Mr. Klein's adoption of traditional English blank verse.

The tone he achieves is dispassionate but forceful. Nowhere is there a hint of the poet anxiously sounding himself and the world for solid ground. But for all his scrupulous directness, Mr. Klein does not fool either himself or his reader into thinking the poet an anonymous infallible centre of perception. His rare cris de coeur are the obverse of lyric outbursts. For example "The Cripples," with such flawless lines as

> How rich, how plumped with blessing is that dome

and

> God mindful of the sparrows on the stairs?

ends with the deliberate monosyllabic dullness of

> And I who in my own flesh once had faith like this
> but have not now, am crippled more than they.

This ability to see and speak himself as simply and accurately as any other part of experience makes "Portrait of the Poet as Landscape" a great poem. One cannot read it without wanting to see it ranged squarely beside Auden's best.

The same mature and acid tolerance distinguishes the portrait pieces, for example "M. Bertrand" ("Oh but in France they arrange these things much better") and "M. Gaston" ("You remember the big Gaston for whom everyone predicted a bad end?"). The sadness that lies behind such insight is expressed directly in "Université de Montréal" with its luminous perspective of overpassed centuries, or in "The Green Old Age" where all living resonance is gone into bluntness.

All the poems in this collection have Canadian themes. And in our day which disposes of three hundred miles in an hour, it is good to have the reassurance that the poet's world at least is not shrinking, and that his homeland is a human environment, not a preserve of sovereignty. In fact wherever its context remains wholly Canadian—"The Rocking Chair" or "Spinning Wheel" for instance—the poetry is a little dreary. The real excitement starts when the sugar maple is translated through shifts of fine metaphor, until it is certainly no longer the familiar national symbol the pious serve at last,

> thanking those saints for syrops of their dying
> and blessing the sweetness of their sacrifice;

or again, when the grain elevator of the West stands out in a rich Oriental setting—the river's "white Caucasian sleep," the grains "Mongolian and crowded":

> for here, as in a Josephdream, bow down
> the sheaves, the grains, the scruples of the sun
> garnered for darkness; and Saskatchewan
> is rolled like a rug of a thick and golden thread.

So Mr. Klein can speak of Canada and sound the note that wakens vibrations through all times and places. May he publish soon a handsome volume cumulating all his work to date and including those facsimile pages.

Canadian Comment

John Sutherland

This review appeared in Northern Review, *Vol. II (1949), pp. 30-34, the magazine which succeeded* First Statement. *It is reprinted here by permission of the Estate of John Sutherland.*

Sutherland praises (with some qualifications) the new technical resources of Klein's poems and the deeper awareness revealed in "Political Meeting."

The Rocking Chair and Other Poems, recently awarded the Governor General's Medal, is A. M. Klein's fourth book and easily his best. One of the most interesting poems is the "Portrait of the Poet as Landscape," originally published in "First Statement" and preceding in time the majority of the poems in this collection. It is interesting because it is in effect Klein's only statement of poetic intention since *Hath Not A Jew,* and it corrects that nose-dive into antiquity by realizing the poet in his contemporary setting. Successful as an objective study, balancing satire with an oblique defence, it is also a personal poem in which the author acknowledges kinship with the "relicts" who, rejected by modern society, "make . . . haloes of their anonymity." It is the personal element that is important in the creative result. In this "Portrait of the Poet" we first encounter the more subtle analysis and the contemporary techniques that characterize the work published in the present book.

When "Portrait of the Poet" was written in the early Forties, Klein was associated with the Montreal *Preview* group and his new poems reflect their blending of Auden and Thomas. Occasionally we meet Auden face to face, as in the re-writing of "The Unknown Citizen" in the first section of the "Portrait of the Poet" ("nobody, it appears, missed him enough to report"), or in the conclusion of the third section

> . . . desire affection, private and public loves;
> are friendly and then quarrel and surmise
> the secret perversions of each other's lives.

More often we find the telegraphic style, the juxtaposition of abstract and concrete nouns, the mirror images and the Auden key words "lonely" and "private," "hero," "guilt" and "loss." From Auden through Page and Anderson comes the second "shock of belated seeing":

> the lonelinesses peering from the eyes of crowds;
> the integers of thought, the cube-roots of feeling . . . .

In the Rocking Chair and Other Poems there is an increased awareness of the individual as integer and type—the conjunction of the private loneliness and the crowd—and a discreet use of psychoanalytic techniques.

From Auden the "mirroring lenses forgotten on a brow . . . that shine with the guilt of their unnoticed world": from Thomas

> the torso verb, the beautiful form of the noun
> and all those shaped and warm auxiliaries . . .

or a way of making the lenses sparkle and glow. From Auden the identity of the individual and his surroundings, reduced to intellectual order: from Thomas the identity felt and experienced in intimate, physical terms "until no join is seen between flesh and flesh . . . between hair and grass" (the quotation is from Patrick Anderson's "Summer's Joe"). The deliberate congestion of rime, part-rime

and assonance, of liquids and sibilants, suggests Hopkins
as seen through Thomas:

> Upon the ecstatic diving board the diver,
> poised for parabolas, lets go
> lets go his manshape to become a bird.
> Is bird, and topsy-turvy
> the pool floats overhead, and the white tiles snow
> their crazy hexagons. Is dolphin. Then
> is plant with lilies bursting from his heels.
>
> . . . .
>
> His thighs are a shoal of fishes: scattered: he
> turns with many gloves of greeting
> towards the sunnier water and the tiles.

Such music shines the glass of self until the self is one with
its reflection. And so the hero with the private wish comes
into his own.

But Thomas' influence is less direct than Auden's and
neither is left unabsorbed in the poetry as a whole. Auden
and Thomas serve as midwives enabling Klein to fuse the
sometimes disparate intellectual and sensuous aspects of
his work. His first book, *Hath Not A Jew,* established him
as a lyrical ironist who was sometimes obtrusively sweet
or bitter but succeeded in several poems in striking the
balance between sentiment and his satiric talent. *Poems*
(1944), published after *The Hitleriad* but containing the
rewritings and tag-ends of *Hath Not A Jew,* showed at
least a temporary failing of the Jewish theme and of the
lyricism. In *The Hitleriad* and such poems as "Pawnshop"
and "In Memoriam," with which Klein's work entered a
second phase, there was a new, bitter satire, a more
marked social and intellectual consciousness, and technically a shift from light riming stanzas to heavy couplets or
stanzaic blocks of architectural pentameters. With the
exception of some pen-portraits in *The Hitleriad* these
poems were both dull and directionless: yet it is clear from

this distance that they represented part of a maturing
process. For in *The Rocking Chair and Other Poems*, with
its re-discovery of the sensuous world, Klein achieves a
new, more intense lyricism fortified by sophistication and
a tough logic. With the joining of the two main strands
in his development he finds a richer and fuller expression
than before.

That does not mean that there are no unsuccessful
poems in the collection. There are weak poems such as
"The Sugaring," whose failure is exaggerated because
Klein is sometimes tempted to force his theme and reluctant to abandon any poem once begun. When he cannot
persuade his reader he buries him in rhetoric:

> O, out of this calvary Canadian comes bliss,
> savour and saving images of holy things,
> a sugared metamorphosis!
> Ichor of dulcitude
> shaping sweet relics, crystalled spotlessness!

Is the reader stubborn? Then bury him in polysyllables,
riddle him with consonants, bisect his skill with exclamation marks!

But the number of successful poems in this book is
proportionately very large, and the number that are more
than just successful is considerable. Among the latter group
I would put "The Rocking Chair," "Frigidaire," "Dress
Manufacturer: Fisherman" and "The Break-Up." I would
also include the wonderfully moving description, "Winter
Night: Mount Royal," "Monsieur Gaston" and the "Portrait of the Poet as Landscape," and I would be tempted to
add "Lone Bather" and "Filles Majeures." If I had to
choose the one poem that impressed me most it would be
"Political Meeting."

For one thing, "Political Meeting" enables us to see in
perspective the relationship between the Klein of *The
Rocking Chair* and of *Hath Not A Jew*. Like some of the
best of the new poems, this sketch of Montreal's mayor

demonstrates the talent for portraiture which distinguished *Hath Not A Jew* and kept alive the mid-period satire *The Hitleriad*.

There is a similarity between the Elijah who made the children laugh while he led them on to a "wonderful synagogue" and this Orator who hides his serious purpose with "wonderful moods" and "tricks" which sometimes extends even to detail (Elijah "pranced like a bear" and the mayor "makes bear's compliments"), and there is a similar blend of sentiment and irony in both poems, focusing first on the antics of these "country uncles" and then shifting to the contrast between their clowning and their deeper purpose. But "Political Meeting" is an achievement superior to "Elijah" or to any poem in *Hath Not A Jew*. The literary influences in *The Rocking Chair and Other Poems,* present here in musical overtones or in turns of phrase ("the hall is yellow with light, and *jocular*" and so on) help to sharpen the wit and give warmth and movement to the poem. They are never used to distort reality, as such influences so often are, and they are firmly balanced by the selection and arrangement of colloquial detail:

> Worshipped and loved, their favourite visitor,
> a country uncle with sunflower seeds in his pockets,
> full of wonderful moods, tricks, imitative talk,
>
> he is their idol: like themselves, not handsome,
> not snobbish, not of the *Grande Allee! Un homme*!
> Intimate, informal, he makes bear's compliments
>
> to the ladies; is gallant; and grins;
> goes for the balloon, his opposition, with pins.

It is this re-creation of the commonplace in the form of portraiture that Klein does best, a fact which may have been evident from *Hath Not A Jew* but which is only now being confirmed.

"Political Meeting" adds another dimension to the portrait in this book of the French Canada which Klein is sometimes tempted to sentimentalize into a "candy-coloured world." Other poems may suggest the oppressive weight of French Canada's history or the oppressive nature of forces bearing on Quebec from the outside world; but still they hang out a placard reading "No one over 16 allowed" and depicting a French Canadian who is the victim of naiveté ("Spinning Wheel") or of second childhood ("The Rocking Chair") or of endless ogreish children who devour every adult in sight ("Annual Banquet: Chambre de Commerce"). In "Political Meeting," on the other hand, we find two main images nicely played against each other: the picture of the kindergarten race in passages such as the one quoted above, and the other and grimmer side of the picture that is interjected warningly here and there through the early stanzas of the poem ("the agonized Y initials their faith," ". . . the scarecrow thing /that shouts to thousands the echoing/of their own wishes") and that mounts in intensity through the final stanzas, giving the poem a new height and depth until the sultry conclusion ". . . and in the darkness rises/the body-odour of race." Through the poem the theme of martyrdom is subtly suggested by "the agonized Y," the line, "Outside, in the dark, the street is *body*-tall," the mass identification with the Christ image in the conclusion "The whole street wears *one face*/shadowed and grim" and the repeated cry of the anti-conscriptionist orator, "*Where are your sons?*" The restraints imposed upon the French-Canadians by their religion, the poet implies, accumulate those feelings of self pity and resentment to which the orator appeals with his agonized refrain.

Klein has always been preoccupied by this theme of martyrdom. But in "Political Meeting," perhaps because he is concerned with another people than his own, he examines the subconscious motives that may intensify the sense of martyrdom produced by an external situation. Partly for this reason, the poem has a depth of meaning that is lacking in the Jewish poems. It gains a further intensity by bringing together the dominant images of Klein's work—the images of the martyr and the clown—and so focusing the conflict in the poet between his intellect and the beliefs of his own people. To bolt orthodoxy whole, is more than the poet can do; yet he laments the poverty of his unbelief (as he does in "The Cripples"), and he cannot let go. The poetic irony is produced by this unresolved situation. It is at once a means of escaping from orthodox belief and of softening its rigidities to make them more acceptable. The poetry revolves on the need "to make a pleasure out of repeated pain," using laughter to lighten the pressures created both by the strictures of faith and the energies required to guard them from attack.

If we can understand Klein's vitality in these terms, we can also appreciate his limitations. The conflict may be by-passed on the emotional level—through the memories of boyhood and their symbolic identification with the French-Canadian world—but it remains unresolved and is seldom touched on directly. Thus, while it would be untrue to say that the poetry lacked a backbone of values, it must be admitted that its structure is ambiguous and dim. We are aware both that Klein is writing out of a tradition and defending himself against it.

Canadian writing may be too solemn as a rule but some of our best writers have been humorists. We have had a number of country uncles in Canadian prose—beginning with Haliburton and coming down to Leacock and Robert Fontaine—and something of their spirt is reflected in the poetry of Klein, Pratt and MacKay. To understand the reason we need go no further than Klein's "Political Meeting." For, after all, the picture there of French Canada is true of puritan Canada generally, and the conflict it reveals in the poet has its counterpart in other Canadian writers. Our cheeks are bound to glow in the puritanical north. We laugh because we are so deadly serious.

A. M. Klein

Louis Dudek

This article appeared in The Canadian Forum, *Vol. XXX (1950), pp. 10-12, and is reprinted by permission of the author. Mr. Dudek has recently made minor revisions in order to improve the style but has not altered the fundamental argument.*

Louis Dudek is well-known as a poet, critic, editor and teacher at McGill University. Like John Sutherland, he offered Klein more than the merely impressionistic appreciation he was usually accorded. There is here a balanced assessment of Klein's successes and failures. Dudek remarks of Klein: "One feels that he can see beyond any criticism made of him, just as he saw beyond his critics in the Thirties."

A. M. Klein, Canadian poet, is probably one of the warmest and kindliest human beings living in this country. Before thinking of his poetry, one thinks of him as a person. There is a shyness about him and a simplicity which he makes an effort to conceal; something one feels, that might be easily bruised. But he has learned to live in the world: he is an active and successful man of affairs. In private, he is a great talker, humorous and always stimulating. He glows with sympathy and with every kind of enthusiasm. And in his best nature, he would not hurt a fly. Once, when asked to join a campaign of war on Canadian sentimental poetry (on the C.A.A.), he smiled shyly and retreated: he had "no desire to hurt kind old ladies." This is our A. M. Klein in Montreal, as we know him.

To the outside world, he is one of Canada's foremost poets—one of the two or three who, as the custom is, would be chosen as representative of all the rest. There are good reasons for this. With those who understand poetry, he does Canada credit. He is an important ambassador.

But there are no doubt readers even in Canada, who will ask: Who is A. M. Klein? What is his history? What has he written? The best answer of course is to be found in Klein's books and printed poems. He is the most autobiographical poet writing in Canada, and he tells us, gradually, almost everything that matters about himself. If he omits some dates and details (unpoetical things), they are easily supplied. He was born in 1909, four years before the First World War. His father, so W. E. Collin says, "was by profession really a potter." We are willing to accept that; but potters by profession in the twentieth century have a hard time of it. Klein intimates in his poetry that his family was poor. He went to schools in Montreal, learning in a pious home and in a parochial school the rudiments of Hebrew religion; in public school, the rudiments of race prejudice, arithmetic, and so forth. He went later to McGill University; graduated with a B.A.; and then continued at the University of Montreal, studying law. He was admitted to the bar in 1933. In the meantime he had published poems in college publications, in *Poetry, a Magazine of Verse* (Oct. 1929), in *The Canadian Forum* (1931 and after), and in a Jewish publication, in the *Menorah Journal*, and a few other places. Since then he has been a practicing lawyer in Montreal—with the firm of "Chat and Klein" of St. James Street, Montreal—and at the same time publishing poetry in most of our local literary magazines and in a few abroad. He has been a candidate for office in Montreal for the CCF Party; and an editor of a periodical, the *Canadian Jewish Chronicle*. At the close of the war, he taught for a few years at McGill University, as guest lecturer in modern poetry. (He didn't enjoy it after the first year: he said he was bothered by "having to repeat the same things.") He is a happily married man, and a father—I do not know at the moment of how large a family. He has had four books published, three by American publishers and one, the most recent, by the Ryerson Press in Toronto. These important books are: *Hath Not A Jew* (1940), *Poems* (1944), *The Hitleriad* (1944), and *The Rocking Chair and Other Poems* (1948). He is now completing an analytical commentary on James Joyce's *Ulysses*.

A circumstance of Klein's development as a poet is revealed by the dates of his published books. In Canada—as everywhere else perhaps in these high-cost-of-printing days, when there is no "great audience" to make "great poets"—a poet will wait ten years with a manuscript on his hands, and when it appears the book does not represent him to the public as he is but as he was. A good part of *Hath Not A Jew* (1940) was written in the early thirties or even before. "Greeting on this Day," Klein has said, was written in 1929 (his twentieth year), following riots in Palestine; "Out of the Pulver and the Polished Lens" at least earlier than 1931; and the "Ballad of the Dancing Bear" earlier than 1932. A number of other long poems, "Design for Mediaeval Tapestry," the "Portraits of a Minyan" and "Talisman in Seven Shreds" were read by W. E. Collin in 1935; Collin refers to one or two of them in *The White Savannahs*. This chronology reveals that Klein's religious poetry belongs to his earliest stage of development, to the late '20s and early 1930s. No doubt he can return to his origins; but Klein's growth has been away from the Hebrew religious core of his poetry toward a realistic and cosmopolitan view of things: and he had advanced some ten years in this direction by the time his first book was published in 1940.

As one divides the work of poets into "periods," Klein has so far had three—his fourth and best, one should hope, still to come: first, the religious, traditional, unquestioning period of his early twenties, ending about 1932; then the period of the World Depression, when he was aping T. S. Eliot and writing Marxist satires; and finally, the period of the '40s, the Second World War, the contact with new Montreal magazines and ideas.

The youthful innocence of Klein's earliest poetry is something he has never altogether lost; it is a quality that readers may miss if they approach him with the prejudice that "modern poetry" is difficult or learned. It is exciting to go back to *Poetry* magazine in 1929, when it was still edited by the genteel Harriet Monroe, to Klein's first important published poem. This is a sequence of brief love poems telling a story, his own in disguise, as Klein is inclined to do:

> Kisses of mine which lent a grace
> To summer, run a frozen race:
> Snowflake-kissing all my face.

Klein's poetry in the early 30s is the exotic product of his reading in Jewish history and religion. Inspired by his father, he had dreamed early of becoming a rabbi. The frustration of this boyhood aspiration, as well as the "normal" conflicts which every Jew experiences in a Christian society, produced a poetry of clowning satire and learned caricature—a rare mixture which ought to amuse and interest the reader, but not bewilder him. It is not necessary to go through a rabbinical course to understand Klein. If one made humorous, lively rhymes about Santa Claus, or say comic poetry on the fantastic lives of Christian Saints, it would be the equivalent of Klein's versification of Hebrew lore and learning in *Hath Not A Jew*. This is religious poetry, illuminated by the shining image of his father, the father-image of Hamlet's piercing cry: "My father, in his habit as he lived!" The religious emotions, however, are not a response to the demands of a whole personality, but the idealism of a growing mind, a romantic expression of boyhood loves.

The form and diction of this early poetry is hardly commendable. The chief influence is that of Shakespeare; but there is also a little Keats, a little Byron; some Heine, probably through Yiddish poetry derived from Heine; add —nursery rhymes and Henry Wordsworth Longfellow. The archaic rhetoric of Shakespeare which Klein adopted is intended to suggest the Jewishness of his themes; and in fact it is possible to think of Elizabethan English as more like Jewish or Latin than sober Christian speech; but this language experiment of Klein's—really a private language— cannot be called a success. It is when he accidentally quits his turgid rhetoric that he is most successful. Some of his words, one feels, are seen in print for the first and last time: "farewelled," "nihility," "insignificantest," "maieutically." As for "beautified," which occurs in *Poems*, Shakespeare himself called that "an ill phrase, a vile phrase, 'beautified' is a vile phrase."

The depression of the '30s ushered in Klein's Eliotesque period of development. This stage represents a break with youth and simple piety, and introduces an angry concern with the harsh facts before everyone's eyes. The principal poem which determined Klein's style in this transition is Eliot's "Prufrock," not *The Waste Land* or *Ash Wednesday*. The result may be studied in Klein's poems published in the *Canadian Forum* in the '30s: "The Diary of Abraham Segal, Poet" (May, 1932); "The Soirée of Velvel Kleinberger" (Aug. 1932); "Blueprint for a Monument of War" (Sept. 1937); "Of Castles in Spain" (June 1938); and "Barricade Smith: His Speeches" (Nov. 1938). Significantly, none of these longish poems have been reprinted in Klein's books: they are a kind of anti-poetry which is necessary to the poet if he is to break out of the hermetic glass in which one writes about Hillel, Abraham, Palestine my own; and the dreams of boyhood.

Klein's imitation of Eliot is obvious and poorly assimilated: "O I have known them all. . . ." "My life lies on a tray of cigarette-butts. . . ." "Madame Yolanda rubs the/

foggy crystal. . . ." Klein, moreover, was using Eliot's delicate anguish to express the hammering certainties of Karl Marx:

> For I have heard these things from teachers
> With dirty hands and hungry features.

All this is part of the move to the left which was so inevitable in the '30s. Stephen Spender has said that the Spanish Civil War was the turning point (note Klein's "Of Castles in Spain"), after which the liberal Left ceased to be a unified anti-fascist movement and has turned toward vigorous varieties of personal salvation. The persecution of the Jews under Hitler, however, forced Klein deeper than ever into the political subject, with the long satire in Popean couplets, *The Hitleriad* (New Directions, 1944). This poem—I think of it as the "hilariad"—is really a commendable failure. True, we once admired it, and it has been praised strongly by E. J. Pratt and faintly by other critics; but beside the bad rhyming and diction and the crude satire, the poem, considering the implications of the subject, has no density or weight of thought. Klein seems to have believed that a strong line against Hitler from the start would have made all things well. We know now that the problem of totalitarianism and world freedom is more difficult, more deeply involved with the age of the masses, with history, with the power of science: an inhuman machine is rolling remorselessly toward us in spite of our liberal intelligence and protests. We do not know the answers to these problems; but in the '30s, the liberal, and Klein also, believed that they knew the answer.

The latest and most complex stage of Klein's poetical development began in the early '40s, and its results so far are represented in the recent Governor General's Award book *The Rocking Chair and Other Poems*. Several causes have operated to make a radical change in Klein's poetry: first, the literary activity in Montreal during the war years, in the magazines *Preview* and *First Statement* (now

Northern Review); then, the specific influence of Patrick
Anderson, and perhaps Irving Layton (compare Layton's
"The Swimmer" with Klein's "Lone Bather"); and third,
an active contact with a wider field of literature through
his teaching at McGill University, especially in reading
Hopkins, James Joyce, Karl Shapiro, and recent poets.
This may seem like a barrage of "influences"; but they are
essential, and they served to stimulate Klein in a direction
he was bound to take.

The Rocking Chair and Other Poems is a fascinating
and readable book, even when one is unhappy with it as
finished poetry. This has always been true of Klein; he has
been vital and stimulating, but never completely satisfying
as a poet.

What Klein is working towards in his recent poetry,
seems to be a greater expertness in the use of varied
poetical tools, especially the techniques of modernism;
greater complexity of ideas and sharpness of images; and
in general an artistic sophistication of attitude somewhat
new in Canada. These have for long been central aims in
modern poetry (other poets in Canada also have these
aims, especially the new poets in Toronto); they are difficult aims; and there can be no claim that Klein has
completely filled them. In some of his verses—"Annual
Banquet: Chamber of Commerce"—he is in fact still at the
point which Pound and Eliot reached in 1915. But in
other poems he moves forward—almost touches something
exciting and new.

Now, it will be said (has been said) that in this new
book Klein has replaced his earlier jargon of Elizabethan
rhetoric with the equally artificial garboils of modern
poetry. That is partly true. The principal weakness in
Klein's poetry has always been his language. This is
peculiarly unfortunate. From the first, he has tended to
experiment with language and develop a speech of his
own; his recent interest in Ulysses is a late effect of this
bent of mind. At the same time he has been able to write

clean and lucid English prose: from "Beggars I have known" in *The Canadian Forum,* June 1936, to the amazing article on criticism in *Here and Now,* No. 4. We know that this deliberate interest in language is characteristic of our century; it has something to do with the disrupted nature of private and social experience, with the unfixed and searching character of poetry itself, with the unreality of the realities in which we live. Joyce, Gertrude Stein, Cummings, have displayed a genius for breaking language and putting its parts into a personal, beautiful order. These experiments are nothing new in literature, since Whitman called the *Leaves of Grass* "a language experiment," and before him the *Lyrical Ballads, Paradise Lost* and *The Fairie Queene* were also of this kind. Klein therefore is in a great tradition, and in good modern company. He has been doing something that Canada badly needs: making new things with old tools, discovering the vast possibilities of poetry. What he has lacked is the criticism and understanding which would let him know when he has succeeded in this type of thing, when he has failed. His experimental poetry is exciting because it is experimental; but it is often below standard as poetry of this kind. Therefore it is often below standard simply as poetry. There are, however, perhaps only half a dozen readers in Canada who are willing to distinguish between the great merit of attempting something new and the failure of achieving it.

Again, the attempt in Klein's latest book to express "Canadianism" through the artifacts of Canadian life—whether a "Spinning Wheel," a "Grain Elevator," a "Frigidaire" or an "Indian Reservation"—is certainly a program of a low order for a poet. There is something obvious, even crudely materialistic about such an attempt; and I imagine that Klein was more Canadian when he wrote about his white-haired father than when he is writing about the dark-haired French-Canadian.

However, the shortcomings of Klein's recent poetry are in themselves the heralds of a new morn. He is now com-

ing into the full strength of his powers: and he is only in
his fortieth year. One feels that he can see beyond any
criticism made of him, just as he saw beyond his critics in
the '30s. His development, however, which is really the
development typical of a young artist, a provincial, has
been slow. What has been twenty years in happening
should have happened in five or six—as it would have done
in Paris, London, or any other large cultural centre.
Canada's infancy is nowhere more clearly revealed than in
this.

And yet we have from Klein to date no less than six or
seven poems as perfect in their kind as poems ever come—
"Reb Abraham," "The Ballad of the Dancing Bear," "I
am weak before the wind . . .," "Psalm VIII," "Psalm
XXVII," the conclusion of *The Hitleriad* and "Lookout:
Mount Royal"—poems that will last as long as Canadian
poetry has readers. He has given us lines and images in his
other poems that stay and return in the memory. What
more do most poets give? What more did John Keats? Or
"Marlowe of the four good lines"?

Allen Mendelbaum

Reprinted from "Everyman on Babylon's Shore," *a review of* The Second Scroll *which appeared in* Commentary, *Vol. XII (1951), pp. 602-604; by permission of the author.*

Like those of Maurice Samuel and Harvey Swados, it reflects the interest of American Jewish intellectuals in the foundation of Israel and in the possibility of a new "Jewish" literature in English. Mr. Mendelbaum is somewhat more aware of the unevenness of execution of the novel than is his colleague. I have omitted a detailed summary of the plot.

The present work by A. M. Klein is a novel, travel book, personal memoir, history-biography of the Jew as wanderer, confession of faith, and work of love. This multiplicity marks the ambitiousness of *The Second Scroll* and its impressiveness; no other Jewish writer in English has attempted to give symbolic—as against episodic—form to so much Jewish experience. And where Klein fails, his failures are themselves significant; for in casting up before us experimental images of the Jew, Klein—even in nostalgia, frizziness, or inadequacy of insight—is Everyman on Babylon's shore. Klein is drenched with *galut,* but curiously un-Western; longs for the exotic, but is revolted by its realms; rises to magnificent prose and stumbles to Corwin rhetoric; is more capable of irony than the unsuspecting might divine, but falls into the mantrap of bathos; knows where his heart is, and articulates seldom with his head.

The work, in short, is an intimate portrait of one who is

certain that Jerusalem is not a place but a people, and also
that Safed is somewhat closer to it than New York or Montreal—but one, too, who is not quite able to convince us
that Jerusalem really *is*. Klein's symbolic mentors are Joyce
and the Rabbis (not rabbis), but where Joyce lifted the
Irish into world literature (as Gogol did the Russians) by
eyeing them remorselessly, Klein attempts the same for the
Jews through love, a mighty lever indeed, but in this book
not always enough.

Klein's chief instruments of condensation are a "plot"
that superimposes, on one narrative line, many places and
many meanings, and a hero, the Jew, who is protean
enough to accommodate hell and heaven in less than two
hundred pages. The narrative line follows the Pentateuch,
with one chapter for each book.

. . . .

The five chapters are parables on the passing scenes of
history. Rome echoes Titus; Casablanca, Moorish Spain;
Safed, ages on end. The ephemeral hero is, as Melech
("King"), David's son, the Anointed One (whose modern
oil is the gasoline)—the sought-after Messiah; and as *ilui*,
Bolshevik, near-Catholic, Cabalist—the seeker of Messiahs.
In concealing Melech's living face, and filtering him
through to us by indirection, A.M. charts his own quest.
But it is a quest deficient in drama, because A.M. himself
is only nominally seeking. He is, essentially, always at one
with his Fathers, and little of Melech's struggle with other
ideas and salvation is Klein's.

Not that the prose, in its heightened and inflated tone,
echoing the Joyce of the Sirens or the Cyclops episode in
Ulysses, is without humour and detachment. Klein's irony
may be heavy at times, but it is there, not only in his style
but in his use of symbolic motifs. The substitution of gasoline for oil denotes not only the presence, but the absence,
of God. Nor does Klein lack a critical eye. His pages on
contemporary Hebrew poetry, on Uri Zvi Greenberg and

Nathan Alterman, are intelligent and perceptive. But the final scene, with the narator saying *Kaddish* over the body of the dead Melech, and its fluid catalogue of the tribes of Israel, is too like a sentimental gathering of the clans. And the appendices that follow do little—except in one case—to help the book.

These long appendices form a second scroll to *The Second Scroll*; they are five glosses (one for each chapter), two from the pen of A.M., three by Melech.

The gloss for "Genesis" is "Autobiographical," a poem evoking the golden age of A.M.'s childhood in Montreal. But Klein's "Hebrew violins/Sobbing delight upon their eastern notes," or "Love leading a brave child/Through childhood's ogred corridors, unfear'd," or ". . . my sadness in remembered joy/Constrictive of my throat," lapse into movie-poetry—if Hollywood were seeking verbal equivalents for movie-music.

The second gloss is a premature elegy for Melech as embodying European Jewry. At its best, the poem is reminiscent of Hart Crane's diction and extravagance, and in its wrathful denunciation of those who slaughtered God's own recalls Tchernichowski's "Zot T'Hi Nikmasenu", or the pentateuchal *tochecha* (commination). It is too long a poem, however, to sustain the emotion that in Milton's "Avenge, O Lord, thy slaughtered saints" suffices for a sonnet.

Gloss three is the richest and most effective. It is an excerpt from a letter written by Melech, "On First Seeing the Ceiling of the Sistine Chapel," to the Monsignor who awaits his conversion. In ornate prose, Melech, confronted by magnificence, describes his vision of the Michelangelo paintings as a hieroglyphic prophecy of the bestiality to which Christian civilization will sink, and an assurance of man's redemption, signaled now for Melech in Israel's survival.

The fourth gloss, a play written by Melech in Casablanca, urging upon the Arab fellowship with the Jew, descends, I feel, to pious homiletics at too many points to leave many readers comfortable.

In the last gloss, sections of a liturgy composed by Melech, there is some worthy devotional poetry, but much of its worth, and even its excitement, reminds me of A.M.'s own previous comments on the Orthodox poets: "Their theme a continual backward-glancing to the past and their technique a pedantry of allusiveness, their work was of Moses mosaic, a liturgy, God's poetry, which is to say poetry for the Most Merciful of Readers."

Klein's reliance on incantation, nostalgia, and exclamation points may not be out of order (perhaps he does have a miracle to shout about); and the texture of his work is never thin. When he writes well, he writes very well; and his love for his matter, Jews, has so little pretension in it, so much good will, that it becomes contagious. Sometimes, however, the task of the reader and the writer is to escape contagion. Fewer catalogues and more precision, less celebration, more dramatic precision and self-examination— less, in short, of what Klein does only too readily and effectively, and more of what he neglects—would strengthen his work. But that work, even as it stands, is a uniquely rich document in the library of Jewish literature in English, one of the few works in this tradition that belong also to modern literature.

The Book of the Miracle

Maurice Samuel

This article appeared in Jewish Frontier *(November 1951, pp. 11-15) and is reprinted by permission of the author.*
    Mr. Samuel had apparently read The Second Scroll *in manuscript for Alfred E. Knopf, and admired it enormously. He calls it "an important event not simply in English or Anglo-Jewish literature, but in the life of English-speaking Jewry." It is perhaps an ironic commentary on this belief that the only edition of the book now available is that of the New Canadian Library.*

It is a long time since a book has moved me as much as this one to a sense of personal responsibility. I am not referring only to the obligation we all feel to share with as many others as possible a peculiar intellectual delight. Certain principles and perspectives are involved here for Jews and Zionists of the kind who read this magazine, and the book derives a non-literary importance from the illumination it casts on them.

Having begun thus portentously, I am aware of another obligation—to assure the reader that he does not have to approach this book as it were with girded loins. It is not one of those edifying "must" books which yield their rewards only to the laborious and dedicated. Its greatness is, in fact, half concealed by its immediate, irresistible charm; it has a lightness which almost deceives—almost, but not quite, for even the unwariest reader will stop here and there, in the midst of a hearty laugh, or a deep sigh, and exclaim under his breath: "What's that? What's that? I think he's putting something over on me, something important, too. I'll have to come back to this passage." And he will. Meanwhile, however, he is held captive by the narrative and the style.

In short, it is a multiple theme which moves here on a number of levels. On the first level there is a story, *stam a maisseh,* of a Canadian poet, Klein himself, who is commissioned by his publisher to go to Israel and make up an anthology in English translation of the latest Hebrew poets of the Homeland. "Go into the market place," says the publisher, "and get me an Isaiah. Of psalmodists bring me only the best. Cull me a canticle in the fields of En Gedi." (If that is how Canadian publishers speak, I'd like to meet a couple of them.) And Klein takes advantage of the commission to go in search, simultaneously, of a lost Uncle Melech, of Ratno, in the Ukraine. Lost in two senses; for this uncle was once an *Ilui* and a light in Israel, afterwards became a renegade, then turned back, and by devious paths is now on his way to liberated Israel. And the dutiful nephew is in physical pursuit.

This *maisseh,* simple, and moving, and straightforward, is sustained to the end, and always it maintains its hold on the emotions. But somewhere along the line we suddenly perceive that it has become legend, too; it is a universal as well as a particular. The griefs and frustrations of Uncle Melech and Nephew Abe converging on Israel; these are wandering Jews (wanderers in the spirit, too) responding to Isaiah: "And it shall come to pass in that day that the Lord shall set his hand again the second time to recover the remnant of his people, which shall be left, from Assyria, and from Egypt, and from Pathros, and from Cush, and from Elam, and from Shinar, and from the islands of the sea." The anguish of the individual is sublimated into the destiny of a people.

On a third level this sublimation reveals the spirit of the *Galut,* and makes intelligible the humor of the Yiddish-speaking Jew. Surely, you would think, a story so tragic personally, so exalted nationally, must employ throughout a style of overcharged loftiness, must leave the reader exhausted by the experience. Not a bit of it. The book is—fantastic though it sounds—predominantly gay! As gay, in fact, as the tragic stories of Sholem Aleichem. To laugh at misery without posing as a saint, or affecting the Byronic or macabre, is of the essence of Yiddish *Galut* humor. I have not till now seen that essence so limpidly distilled in English.

The writer, a master artificer of the English language (of this more below) himself manages to convey the sense of a *Galut* presence—a multiple Jew. We have here the corybantic gleefulness of the Chassid, the sly irony of the Litvak, the earthiness and sensuousness of the Ukrainian and Roumanian Jew, the penetration and far-ranging allusiveness of the Talmudist, the hints also, not (God forbid) of the *kofer be-ikkar* (renegade), but certainly of one who is at least *a bissel gechapt in der maisseh* (suspect). I must again refer to Sholem Aleichem, and to Tevyeh, the *Galut* Jew *in excelsis*. Only a gloomy religious pedant would read blasphemy into Tevyeh's half-jocular, half-serious exchanges with the Judge of the World. So with Klein's tongue-in-cheek playfulness in matters Jewish. They do not diminish, they heighten, the experience of faith.

The playfulness is Chassidic, whether by origin or association does not matter. It makes plausible the incredible, namely, that there was a thing called delight in Jewishness, even in the darkness of exile (incredible, that is, to the outside world and to assimilated Jews). Klein thus recalls his first Jewish lessons: "The old Tannenbaum, round little pygmy of eighty, bearded to the breastbone, was my teacher, and I recall how it was his custom, as I struggled with the vowel-signs — those beneath the letters, like prompters prompting, those beside the letters, like nudgers nudging, and those on top, like whispers whispering—how it was his custom to urge me forward from each mystic block to the next with repeated promise of pennies from heaven." He tells of Sukkoth and the circling about the *Almemar*: "As every year, the old Kuznetzov was already ecstatically exhilarated; his beard awry, his muddy features shiny pink, his very pockmarks hieratic like unleavened bread, he was dancing—a velvet-mantled scroll in his arms —with a fine, other-worldly abandon, as his friends clapped hands in time."

There are fourth and fifth levels, and still others, (some extraneous to the book!), which beckon, and remain to be investigated. Let these three suffice here. But let it be added that Klein's playfulness, Yiddish-Galut throughout, is nevertheless transferable, therefore universal, and applies itself as effectively to non-Jewish matter.

He thus describes the learned and subtle Monsignor Piersanti of Rome, a Catholic fisher of souls, who had cast his net for the wandering Uncle Melech: "A man full of sympathy and understanding. He had, too, a very courtly manner, was extremely well-read—I got the impression it was his special duty to read all the books on the Index. As we talked of the atrocities which had made lurid our decade, and of the unplumbable depths from which their motives sprang, the Monsignor was double edged with paradox aimed at the easy explanations that both the economists and the psychiatrists had to offer for the world's ills. It was as if he were plucking playfully now a tuft of Marx's beard, now a tuft of Freud's."

Of the sensuous-plastic or earthy side I quote one passage, to which my saliva responded at once without any preconditioning of Pavlov's dog. It is from his description of the fruit market of Casablanca: "Golden oranges of Tetuan, pyramided; navelled, the pomegranates of Marrakech; Meknes quince; the sun sweet inside their little globes, and upon their skins the mist of unforgotten dawns, the royal grapes of Rabat. Even the sheathed onions, mauve, violet, pink, poll-tufted like the warriors of the Atlas, seemed fruit that I had never seen before. And dominating—whether in the smooth, cool round, or, sliced, as crimson little scimitars adorning the Negro smile—were watemelons, miniature Africas, jungle-green without, and within peopled by pygmy blacks set sweetly in their world of flesh."

Most of the foregoing is, frankly, temptation and seduction—emphasis on the sheer readableness of the book, which I must try to establish before going on to its significance. On the other hand, the book would have no significance at all without this dazzling attractiveness. The author would never have been able to convey his intention by mere discourse and description and narrative; only infection is equal to the task. And he intends (among other things) nothing less than to recapture the lyric bliss which the Return inspired in the Prophets.

No paltry ambition this—though one need not accuse the author of having been aware of it in these terms; and the difficulty is pointed by a paradox. There are two dominant beliefs about the singing literature of the Return from Babylon. One, orthodox, proclaims that the verses were anticipation, pure prophecy. There is much to be said for this: anticipation is always more blissful than realization. The other asserts, Higher-Critically, that generations, centuries, had passed, before the Jews realized what a miracle had taken place and the outburst of jubilation came long after Zerubabel, Ezra and Nehemiah had become half legends. In either case, it is clear that no one credits the contemporaries of the miracle with the power to express it; or perhaps even with the sensitivity to be actively aware of it.

To be sure, we are told that when the building of the second temple was begun in Zerubabel's days, "many of the priests and Levites and chiefs of the fathers, who were ancient men, that had seen the first house, when the foundation of this was laid before their eyes, wept with a loud voice; and many shouted aloud for joy. So that the people could not discern the noise of the shout of joy from the noise of the weeping of the people . . ." They were deeply moved by the event, they laughed and wept together. But they had not, it seems, that alertness of response which issues in eternally infectious words. Before or after them, by centuries, the event so penetrated a few visionaries that these, the nonparticipants, were moved to the everlasting verses of redemption; and so it is in Isaiah—strangely enough—that we experience to the depths the meaning of Ezra and Nehemiah.

No doubt the generation which is the worked-on material of a miracle is exhausted by it; nothing is left over for chronicling the experience. This, and not "the need for perspective," as we usually put it, accounts for the absence of singers in the time of action. We, the—often reluctant—material of our contemporaneous miracle of reborn Israel, feel ourselves to be depleted of the sense of wonder. We know that we ought to feel, more consistently, more enduringly than we do, on a higher level, more creatively, the marvel without parallel. Instead, we have fallen into exhaustion, we are querulous, we plod when we ought to leap, we are disappointed, and disappointed with ourselves for feeling disappointed. Well, it is possible that not the least mirculous element in the business is that we carry on, and will continue to carry on, without inspiration.

But here, in Klein's book, a sudden and almost unbelievable reversal has taken place. Here the reward is vouchsafed us against the rules. A man in the midst of the miracle—and he not a brooding spectator, but an actual, sweat-covered fellow-laborer—has released the note of pure joy. And it is so authentic, so uninvolved in doubt, calculation, irritability of partisanship or meanness of the moment, that for an instant we perceive the whole millenial trajectory.

All that I have read hitherto, in several languages, on the miracle, has been forced and transitory—yes, from the Declaration of Independence itself to the latest screech of propaganda. This, it will be obvious from the foregoing, is not a reproach, and not even a complaint. It is the acknowledgement of an all but inevitable condition. And here is sheer delight. *The Second Scroll* sounds off for some prophet of centuries past, undiscovered, or one waiting his turn some centuries hence, unborn. But even as in the Ezra account, we cannot discern the noise of the shout of joy from the noise of the weeping of the people. We of this generation have been the witnesses of a miracle of evil and destruction, as well as of one of grace and creation. There has been no commensurate utterance for the former, any more than for the latter. On this subject, too, I have read widely persistently, professionally, and have resigned myself to what seemed to be the inevitable. In *The Second Scroll* we come nearest to the right word for what happened to six million of us in Europe. And it is so interwoven with the theme of the redemption, its sorrows and terrors are so blended with the singing and rapture of Israel Resurrected, that we put down the book in a daze, and wonder what our feelings really are.

I will not quote in illustration of these assertions. The reader has been given enough to get a measure of the genius of the writing, and more than he deserves if he is not going to get the book.

Since this is not, strictly speaking, a review, it would seem out of place to make more than passing mention of the writer's peculiar style. This is far from the case. It so happens that Klein's management of English has certain implications beyond, or in addition to, a consideration of English literature.

I have said that he is a master craftsman. His assiduous and diligent enjoyment of the word as such comes from an immensely sophisticated knowledge of its structure and history. No one who reads this book is surprised to learn that he is a student and interpreter of James Joyce. Structurally, too, *The Second Scroll* has an affinity with the elaborate Joycean technique of symbolism: but of this nothing more will be said here. Except that, from where

I stand, those special merits of the book are so much gravy. What Klein has done with English is, roughly, break it down in order to introduce a coloration of his own—of ours, in fact. He does not get down, as Joyce does, to the actual fragmentation of the word itself. It is the style which he disassembles and reassembles with a curious new effect: a new effect which gives us our first intimation of what might be called Judaeo-English.

Again we must take note, at once, of certain implications, to affirm some, deny others. Judaeo-English would be analogous to Judaeo-German (Ur-Yiddish) in that it is the peculiar twist which a Jewish group cultural expression would give to English style. It would *not* be analogous to Judaeo-German in the implication of ghettoization, folkishness and lack of instruction. That is, it would not be East Side English, as caricatured by popular novelists, pushed to an extreme. Far from it. We shall never have in America a Jewish culture, *régionaliste,* indigenous, and yet in our tradition, if we think of separation and privacy. We shall have it, if at all, only as a consequence of complete acceptance of our locale. A Jewish culture in America can exist only in symbiosis with an American culture.

But it comes down to this: whatever may be the case here and there today, whatever individual anachronisms may be found tomorrow, an American Jew, to have Jewish culture at all, must have American culture too. We will never again produce the so-called simple Jewish *Folkmensch*. That was possible only when Jewish life in the diaspora consisted—as Dubnov correctly pointed out—of what were virtually colonies. The Jewish person, carrying the Jewish values, will have to belong to an intellectual élite. And this élite, as a group, will have to sound a note of its own in American culture.

Something of that note we already catch in *The Second Scroll*. Chord is perhaps a better word, for it is a composite. Klein sounds, simultaneously, in harmony, many depths of Western culture and of Jewish knowledge and tradition. Allusions vibrate in the overtones of each note in the chord: here we catch an echo of a Yiddish proverb, there of a Biblical verse, elsewhere of a dispute of the Babylonian academies. For full enjoyment of the book one must have a point to point identity of equipment with the author: Bible and Talmud and modern Hebrew poetry; experience of the *cheder,* the *synagogue,* the public school, the university; recollection of, at least, or contact by home talk with, the last big Jewish subcivilization of Europe: acquaintance by reading with recent history, and acquaintance by participation with the making of the Jewish State. But also, a deep-grounded love of the English language, of parts of its vast literature, an organic—not provisional—self-identification with the spiritual struggles of the west.

It is asking a great deal—but not by traditional Jewish standards. Judaism was always exemplified, at centre, by an intellectual élite, and in the mass a recognition existed, and nostalgia for membership. Not here is the main difficulty with this concept of our culture in the west, but a doubt as to the *historic* feasibility of such a long-range spiritual enterprise.

It will, however, seem a little less formidable, historically speaking, if we see it thus: in all advanced countries there rise from time to time cultural groups which have their own atmosphere and tonality (e.g. the New England Transcendentalists). No one challenges them as an abberation or doubts their value. They have their day, they disappear. Their impermanence is due to their topicality; they deal perhaps with eternal problems, but it is in a temporal idiom. The possibility that a Jewish group of this kind can acquire permanence is based on the durability of the manifold idioms it uses and lives by: of religion, of history, of endogamy, and of a feeling of destiny.

The literary idiom of that Jewish culture in the West is yet to be created; or let me say that it is in process of creation in *The Second Scroll*. And this brings me back to the opening sentence of this statement, concerning the sense of responsibility which the book has awakened in me. If I am at all right—as I think after many rereadings, which began with the manuscript nearly a year ago, and continue in the published volume—we are face to face with an important event not simply in English or Anglo-Jewish literature, but in the life of English-speaking Jewry. The direct, unreflectingly pleasure we derive from the reading of the book should not deflect our attention from this remarkable fact.

Review of *The Second Scroll*

Malcolm Ross

This review of The Second Scroll *appeared in* The
Canadian Forum, *Vol. XXXI (1952), p. 234 and is reprinted by permission of the author.*

*Malcolm Ross is a professor of English and also general
editor of McClelland and Stewart's New Canadian Library
paperback series. In his review he suggests the nature of
Klein's "Canadianism."*

One hears very little nowadays about the respective claims
and merits of the "native" as against the "cosmopolitan"
tradition in Canadian writing. Perhaps this is because it
has dawned on us at last that the tradition native to us is
inescapably cosmopolitan and that, actually, our tradition
is as much before us as it is behind us. We are beginning
to *make* tradition now because it is only now that we have
become aware of what it is that we must make. We have
lately discovered that we are not just a mixed batch of
transplanted Englishmen, Frenchmen, Scots, Jews and
Slavs, but a uniquely structured people with multi-
dimensional cultural possibilities. And we are learning
that the tensions which articulate this unique Canadian
structure are dynamic, positive, creative.

In the light of this new awareness we should be quite
prepared to recognize in A. M. Klein's *The Second Scroll*,
a necessary extension of our range of vision. Klein stakes
out a claim for us in richer and further dimensions of
experience than we have hitherto dared to occupy. But
these dimensions are properly ours. We have only to

inhabit our own domain in order to possess what we
already have.

In his poetry Klein has come close to creating the archetypal Canadian pattern—a dense organic fusion of traditional idiom, ancient myth and cult, the contrapuntal
dialectic of our French-English relationship, the sophisticated technical reach of man alive in this age and in whom
all ages are alive.

The novel, Klein's first, is experimental in form, complex in theme. It is the story of a quest at once personal,
communal and spiritual. The method is that of analogy
and is therefore of a piece with the patterning of diverse
and seemingly discontinuous facts of experience characteristic of Klein's best poetry. Obviously, Klein has been
schooled by Joyce but, perhaps because of the clear, unequivocal religious affirmation of the novel, one is reminded not so much of Joyce as of Dante. The inferno of
pogrom gives way in turn to purgatorial quest, to a realization of the Earthly Paradise of the new Jerusalem, even to
a prospect of the universal and eternal.

In working out his analogical pattern Klein involves
lyric, dramatic and epic modes. The narrator (presumably
the author) is in search of Israel, in search of his fabulous
Uncle Melech, in search of himself. The narrative account
of the journey from Montreal to Israel by way of Rome is
terse reportage illuminated and deepened by an original
use of the footnote. Early in the book after an account of
a European pogrom there is a footnote poem "Autobiographical" in which the eternal persecution of the Jew
is personalized in the loneliness of the Jewish boy in
Montreal—a loneliness which, however, is dignified by a
pride of participation in the destiny of a people. The
lyrical cry is matched and met in other footnotes by frag-
ments of formal drama and brilliant exercises in symbolism
and exegesis. Significantly, the chapters of the narrative
are entitled Genesis, Exodus, Leviticus, Numbers, Deuteronomy: the epic wandering and arrival of the ancient

sacred tribe is recapitulated in the odyssey of the modern
Jew. Uncle Melech's desertion of the law for flirtation
first with communists and then with the Church of Rome,
his enslavement by the Nazis, his escape from the new
"Egypt," his brief vision of the Promised Land—that is,
simultaneously, an account of the plight and the hope of
the Jewish intellectual in our time, an exercise by Klein in
self-analysis, and the unrolling of the *second* scroll, the
repetition and the fulfilment of Mosaic quest and creed.

The book has faults. For one thing it is over-compressed.
While the analogical layers are always held in the grip of
the intellect, while the symbol is always lucid, proper
emotive suggestiveness is sometimes lacking. And there is
a defect of the opposite kind. Sometimes the purple
passage rises with disconcerting abruptness out of the
hardest cerebral rock. One might say that while the skeletal
structure of the book is sound and strong the flesh is
unevenly distributed.

But this is a compelling book and one which gives
Canadians some right to feel adult. The author's Canadianism is a nodal point in the treatment of his theme. In
exploring the final dimension of his spiritual heritage
Klein makes it ours. Talmud and Torah take their place
in our pattern beside the book of Common Prayer, the
Missal, the Institutes. We are enriched. And we acknowledge that the racial memories of our multi-dimensional
culture are much too deep and broad to be filled by
Cartier and Wolfe and the United Empire Loyalists. It
is not the item but the *pattern* which is Canadian. As
persons we live by various and separate spiritual inheritances and loyalties and we preserve our differences. But
at another level as Canadians, we take our life from the
fruitful collision and interpretation of many inheritances.
And thus we grow.

Klein's Drowned Poet: Canadian Variations on an Old Theme

Milton Wilson

Reprinted from "Klein's Drowned Poet: Canadian Variations on an Old Theme," Canadian Literature, *No. 6 (1960), pp. 5-17, by permission of the author.*

Milton Wilson is a critic and professor of English at Trinity College, University of Toronto. For some years he wrote the annual review of Canadian poetry in the University of Toronto Quarterly's *"Letters in Canada" series. His essays on Canadian poetry are always stimulating and suggestive. I regret very much that I was obliged, for reasons of space, to omit the portions of Professor Wilson's article that deal with earlier and later poets than Klein.*

To call Klein and Pratt the poles of Canadian poetry is to suggest something in common as well as a world that holds them apart. Their diction often calls for the same critical adjectives: polysyllabic, technical, erudite, as well as colloquial or prosaic. Before 1940 even their versification might have seemed equally traditional: sometimes neat and sometimes expansive, but never intricate or explosive. The discontinuous narrative forms which start with *The Witches' Brew* and end with *Toward the Last Spike* are the natural companions of the lyrical mosaics of *Hath Not a Jew*. They are both poets of "the beleaguered group." And no doubt in the end Pratt's "apocalyptic dinner" and Klein's "goodly eating / Of roast leviathan" come to the same thing. But, in the meantime, no reader could possibly confuse their wordplay or their quatrains and couplets, not to mention the immediate substance of things seen and hoped for. And to turn from Pratt's pre-war poems to Klein's is suddenly to leave the sea far behind, almost to forget that it ever existed. *Hath Not a Jew* must be the driest book in Canadian poetry. Whatever the swings of the pendulum between Egypt and Promised Land, the poet never gets his feet wet.

In this as in many other ways, Klein's last book of poetry, *The Rocking Chair and Other Poems,* differs from his first. The obvious differences—a new and explicit French-Canadian setting, fresh winds of style blowing through Montreal in the forties—are not necessarily the most valuable. We have been told that the influence of the *Preview* and *First Statement* groups in wartime Montreal served to release Klein, that it allowed him to move from the dead end of *Poems 1944* and the misstep of the *Hitleriad* to the new vitality of his fourth book. But this somewhat factitious shot in the arm had its disadvantages. More poems than "The Provinces" try to compete with Patrick Anderson, and "Les Filles Majeures" is the sort of thing that P. K. Page did much better. The value of the new setting is equally ambiguous. "The Rocking Chair," "The Snowshoers," "The Spinning Wheel" and other poems of the kind are brilliant but very detached; quaint genre-pieces by a contemporary and more elaborate Krieghoff. Klein's eye and ear are more alert than ever, and the book is full of superb exercises; but, although the places and people of Quebec (and occasionally other provinces) are painted in more detail than the towns and sundry folk of *Hath Not a Jew,* they are grasped with less force and concern. In other words, Klein's new regionalism is as much an inhibition as a release.

The richest and probably the best are those poems where Klein's first world seems to interpenetrate his second. He has never written anything lovelier or stronger than "Grain Elevator," besides which (as gloss perhaps) I like to place the best stanza of "Bread":

> O black-bread hemisphere, oblong of rye,
> Crescent and circle of the seeded bun,
> All art is builded on your geometry,
> All science explosive from your captured sun.

Or maybe the best companion poem might be "Quebec Liquor Commission Store." The book is full of such interesting constructions and parodies of constructions: the anti-ark of "Pawnshop" the sound-proof jungle of "Commercial Bank," the "grassy ghetto" of "Indian Reservation," and even "Frigidaire," which compresses within its "slow sensational and secret sight" a whole Laurentian winter pastoral. The interpenetration of worlds and images is sometimes more than a little startling. Anyone who turns from Klein's novel, *The Second Scroll*, back to "Political Meeting" will greet the line "a country uncle with sunflower seeds in his pockets" with a shock of recognition, and for one awful moment see the shadow of Uncle Melech rising up behind the Camillien Houde who is his parody.

The book ends "at the bottom of the sea," but it has gone under water a few times before that. There's a lone bather who seems to be merman, dolphin, water-lily and charioted Neptune all together, although his sea is only a tiled swimming pool. Another poem ends with the rising "from their iced tomb" at break-up time of

> the pyramided fish, the unlockered ships,
> and last year's blue and bloated suicides.

But no catalogue of "immersion images" would prepare anyone for Klein's Lycidas when he finally appears at the beginning of "Portrait of the Poet as Landscape," an Orpheus dismembered into Bartlett's Quotations, buried

on the library shore, unwept even by our brief custodians
of fame.

> Not an editorial writer, bereaved with bartlett,
> mourns him, the shelved Lycidas.
> No actress squeezes a glycerine tear for him.

And that beginning hardly prepares us for his last appearance at the end of the poem, crowned and shining (however equivocally) at the bottom of the sea, another "lost
prince of a diadem."

Klein gives us a good many alternative portraits to
examine on our way to the true one. First we must travel
down the usual elegiac cul-de-sac and test the glory and
the nothing of a name. But fame's spur has never seemed
so blunt; and the series of unholy names (dots, votes,
statistics) manage to suggest nothing less than a grim
parody of the original creative spirit, the blasphemy of a
nameless god:

> O, he who unrolled our culture from his scroll . . .
> who under one name made articulate
> heaven, and under another the seven-circled air,
> is, if he is at all, a number, an x,
> a Mr. Smith in a hotel register.

What John Crowe Ransom once claimed for Milton's elegy
("a poem nearly anonymous") Klein is claiming for
Lycidas himself.

From the poet as name, Klein's portrait-album turns to
the poet as others see him, and, at greater length, as he sees
himself—falling and rising "just like" a poet. His self-
images range from "his mother's miscarriage" at the nadir
to "the Count of Monte Cristo come for his revenge" at
the zenith, or (to reverse the cycle) from an adolescent
first exploring the body of the word to a "convict on
parole" (Klein's puns are inescapable). Then he and his
kind are portrayed as social beings, scattered about the

country, cherishing their esoteric art, joining a political
party, seeking and repelling love, multiplying within,
alone and not alone. The next portrait strikes deep into
Klein: the poet as citizen *manqué,* exile on a reservation.
As if he were literally disinherited, cuckolded, displaced
by someone else, this poet tries to guess his double outside
the poetic ghetto, the man who has come forward to fill
"the shivering vacuums his absence leaves." Then the
album returns to fame in another form: the public personality the poet dreams of, which "has its attractions, but
is not the thing."

Indeed, none of these portraits has much to do with the
poet as writer of poetry, although they may be a clue to
some "stark infelicity" at the bottom of the poetic process.
The last portrait, superimposed on the rest in the sixth
and last section of the poem, is another matter. This poet,
seeding his illusions, is Adam the namer and praiser and
prophet in one. He takes a green inventory, he psalms the
world into existence, and then, from a planet of vantage,
he takes "a single camera view" of the earth, "its total
scope and each afflated tick"—world enough and time
rolled in a book, or (if one remembers the first section)
scroll. By this means, the drowned poet breathes and
pulsates. Each item he praises is "air to his lungs and
pressured blood to his heart" and when the list is complete
he has resurrected his own drowned body as well as the
world's. Or, if this seems too lofty a way of putting it, the
next stanza speaks more simply of renewing the craft of
verse, of bringing new forms and creeds to life, and thereby
of paying back some of the air that is daily being stolen
from his lung.

> These are not mean ambitions. It is already something
> merely to entertain them. Meanwhile, he
> makes of his status as zero a rich garland,
> a halo of his anonymity,
> and lives alone, and in his secret shines
> like phosphorus. At the bottom of the sea.

The phrasing of the last two stanzas is extremely tentative; the garland and halo of heavenly fame share their brightness with the death-blue shine of the corpse; and Lycidas remains waiting "meanwhile." The ending will seem even more negative and ironic if we contrast it with the psalm-followed "drowning instant" at the end of Uncle Melech's liturgy, the last gloss of *The Second Scroll*. Of course, between the poet's multiple-portrait and Uncle Melech's composite photograph lies the establishment of Israel in 1949. But Klein's poem is still fundamentally affirmative. The poet is nobody, a mere cipher; but the zero is also the halo over his drowned head: zero as hero, or "Aught from Naught," as Uncle Melech would have put it. And, although his status as nobody may be his "stark infelicity," it may also be the poet's extinction of personality, the ultimate anonymity behind the ultimate poem. As if to emphasize the affirmative, Klein changed his title from "Portrait of the Poet as Zero" to "Portrait of the Poet as Landscape" and thereby gave his favourite "microcosm-macrocosm" image pride of place.

Some of the details of the poem (the maps and charts, the images of exploration, the drowned body itself) in combination make it seem likely that Klein was remembering one of Donne's best-known hymns. But a reader of Canadian poetry might well be reminded of Klein's own early masterpiece "Out of the Pulver and the Polished Lens." What comes out of Spinoza's lens, as it magnifies one way and shrinks another, is a figure for God's relation to man and nature. Between microcosm and macrocosm stands God, the imminent lens or eye, the focus and burning glass of all creation. Klein's Spinoza translates this figure into theorem and into pantheistic psalm.

I behold thee in all things, and in all things: lo, it is
    myself;
I look into the pupil of thine eye, it is my very countenance
    I see. . . .

The flowers of the field, they are kith and kin to me; the
     lily
my sister, the rose is my blood and flesh. . . .
    Even as the stars in the firmament move, so does my
      inward heart,
and even as the moon draws the tides in the bay, so does
     it the blood in my veins. . . .
    Howbeit, even in dust I am resurrected; and even in
      decay I live again.

Spinoza can reach a similar conclusion through Klein's
alchemical or Cabbalistic images: cirque, skull, crucible,
golden bowl, hourglass, planet, "macrocosm, sinew-shut."
The "horrible atheist" proves "that in the crown of God
we are all gems." The title of this early poem might just
as well be "Portrait of Spinoza as Landscape." One might
even justify calling the later one "Portrait of the Poet as
Lens." Its poet portrait is also a poet-photographer. At first
we are only told of "mirroring lenses forgotten on a brow/
that shine with the guilt of their unnoticed world." But
the last picture to be developed under water is that "single-
camera view": man, world, and maybe burning glass, all
at once. . . .

Poet of a Living Past:
Tradition in Klein's Poetry

M. W. Steinberg

This was one of four articles devoted to various aspects of Klein's work in Canadian Literature, *No. 25 (September 1965). It is reprinted by permission of the author.*

M. W. Steinberg is a professor of English at the University of British Columbia. This article provides a very sound general introduction to Klein's work and the forces that shaped his thought.

CL 25

In "Ave Atque Vale," the opening poem in his first volume of poetry, *Hath Not a Jew* (1940), A. M. Klein states that his intention is to turn to his Jewish heritage, to become, as he said in a later poem, the poet "who unrolled our culture from his scroll." Probably no other major Canadian writer so deliberately and consistently wrote within a tradition. This purpose was all the more easily accomplished, for it was a rich heritage which, existing as a minority culture, was clearly defined and discernible. He was at the same time an intensely personal poet, his awareness and concern with himself probably being reinforced by the realization of the separateness of himself and his tradition in the general social milieu.

The personal element is to be found in the tone and style of his poetry, the flavour of personality that permeates most of what he wrote. The quality of unembarrassed sentimentality—nostalgic, tender, affectionate—usually preserved from excess by simplicity of statement or held in check by light irony; the tone of impassioned indictment or commitment; his whimsical humour; and his enthusiasm as seen, for example, in his delight in festivities or in

expressing his awareness of the divine: all these characterize his work, less tangibly perhaps but as definitely as
his highly individual poetic language. But Klein is personal in a more direct manner. Autobiographical statements are to be found in many poems, from the first poem
in the first volume to the last poem, "Portrait of the Poet
as Landscape," in his fourth and final volume of verse,
The Rocking Chair and Other Poems (1948). He recalls
scenes from his childhood at home, in school and on the
street, the sights and smells of the Montreal Jewish quarter
and the games he played; he reminisces often about his
parents and teachers, who shaped his growth. In *Poems*
(1944), in a sequence of thirty-six poems entitled "The
Psalter of Avram Haktani," Klein describes or alludes to
the major events of his life from his birth through his
marriage. The title makes clear the personal reference in
the poems. It contains an obvious play on his own name,
the word "Haktani" in Hebrew meaning "small" or the
Yiddish and Germanic "klein." These poems disclose his
inmost fears and hopes, thereby revealing many of his
interests and values.

Klein however, for the most part, subordinates the personal element. Even when he is concerned with himself, he
usually sees himself in relation to a continuing tradition,
an attitude which keeps the personal element confined and
yet achieves a kind of enlargement for it by identifying it
with a larger entity. Klein conveys this sense of identification most clearly in "Psalm XXXVI, a Psalm touching
genealogy."

> Not sole was I born, but entire genesis:
> For to the fathers, that begat me, this
> Body is residence. Corpuscular,
> They dwell in my veins, they eavesdrop at my ear,
> They circle, as with Torahs, round my skull,
> In exit and in entrance all day pull
> The latches of my heart, descend, and rise—
> And there look generations through my eyes.

Klein, a learned Jew, has a strong sense of history and his place in it. He is always conscious of himself, as the furthest extension and summation of his people and its heritage. For Klein, as for all traditionalists, the past has an immediacy that makes it a present reality. Furthermore, in Jewish religious teaching, which shaped traditional responses, time is regarded as hallowed, and moments in history, persons and events are exalted. Place, on the other hand, is rarely sanctified and tends to be disregarded. This attitude to place, with its religious basis and significance, has probably been reinforced by the Jewish emphasis on inner experience and by the fact that so much Jewish history has occurred in unwelcomed or tyrannous exile, where no attachment, no deep sense of belonging was possible. In his poetry Klein reflects these traditional attitudes. The sages of Sura and Pumbeditha, Reb Levi Yitschok, or the poet-rabbi Jehuda Ha-Levi are his contemporaries constituting a past that is living for him. Little or no attention is paid in the first three volumes of Klein's poetry to settings. In *The Rocking Chair and Other Poems,* however, Klein does indicate a marked sensitivity to place, whether it be a pawnshop, St. Lawrence Boulevard, or Mount Royal. As in his other relationships, he finds it difficult to maintain any psychic distance from that which he experiences; the places become part of him, and in describing them he becomes very tender and personal. However, Klein's sense of time and of place tend to merge. In fact, he seldom thinks of place without some time referent. Places have history and, as we can see in such poems as "Montreal," "Lookout: Mount Royal," and "The Mountain," it is the history of the place, the events that are associated with it that appeal to him as much as the physical elements, and probably more.

At the core of Klein's traditionalism is his intense religious commitment, a concern that is compounded of an emotional attachment fostered and shaped from his infancy on, both at home and at school; an intellectual attraction

to the challenge of Talmudic debate and the fine-drawn
disquisitory logic of the post-Talmudic scholars; and perhaps most important, the spiritual need for a metaphysic
or a system of beliefs that would order human experience
meaningfully and purposefully and enable him to find
himself in such an order so that he could better understand
this experience, and that would prompt him to reach
beyond the seeming finitudes of time and place—in brief,
to seek God.

In Gloss Aleph of *The Second Scroll*, a poem entitled
"Autobiographical," Klein enumerates many of the vivid
childhood memories that reveal the emotional basis of
his religious attitude. His environment, the Montreal
ghetto, was almost totally Jewish and centred about the
home, the synagogue and the Hebrew school. The outstanding calendar days were the religious festivals, with
the ceremonies and games associated with them. Klein's
attachment to ceremony and ritual is evidenced in the
series of poems "Haggadah" in *Hath Not A Jew*, in the
nuptial psalms in *Poems* and in many affectionate references to the Sabbath and holy day ceremonies at home and
in the synagogue. His parents humbly circumstanced, were
gentle and pious. His brief recollections of them here are
of his mother "blessing candles, Sabbath-flamed" and of his
father telling tales about the famous Chassidic Rabbi, the
Baal Shem Tov. He frequently refers to his parents in his
poems and in nearly every instance the context is some
religious practice or observance and the relationship is one
of love, "Love leading a brave child/Through childhood's
ogred corridors, unfear'd." His references to his childhood
religious teachers reveal the same quality of affectionate
trust and acceptance. To some extent, undoubtedly,
Klein's later religious seeking reflects a somewhat nostalgic
yearning for the relatively simple, secure and abundantly
happy days of his childhood, a seeking in memory for
"The strength and vividness of nonage days." This aspect

of Klein's religious attitude emerges in many poems where, after considering the evils of this nightmare world, he puts his trust in God, a parent-figure, to see him safely through. The imagery in the concluding section of "Reb Levi Yitschok Talks to God" clearly suggests this aspect.

> He raged, he wept. He suddenly went wild
> Begging the Lord to lead him through the fog;
> Reb Levi Yitschok, an ever-querulous child,
> Sitting on God's knees in the synagogue,
> Unanswered even when the sunrise smiled.

The imagery here, however, should not be taken to indicate, as some critics have suggested, an abdication of mature responsibility for a child-like faith in a father-figure, though certainly much of the emotional force stems from such a deeply-rooted association. But Klein is expressing not primarily a desire to escape from the complexities of life, or a personal longing for his earlier simple, protected existence, but rather a traditional Jewish attitude which regards God metaphorically in terms of a homely, intimate, familial relationship, not remote or austere, without confusing the metaphor with the reality.

Klein's studies in Jewish law and philosophy continued after he graduated from Hebrew school in Montreal and even long after he abandoned his intention to enter a seminary to study for the rabbinate. He draws on his learning for his abundant—perhaps over-abundant—references to Biblical and post-Biblical figures, and for the historical events and legends on which he builds many of his poems. The poems in "Talisman in Seven Shreds" (*Hath Not A Jew*), and in "A Voice Was Heard in Ramah" and "Yehuda Ha-Levi, His Pilgrimage" (both in *Poems*) illustrate not only Klein's scholarship but also his ability to discover the relevance of history and tradition to contemporary circumstances. Through these allusions Klein indi-

cates clearly his intellectual attachment to the Jewish
religious heritage. In the opening poem of his first volume,
Hath Not A Jew, Klein emphasizes that when he turns
from his cosmopolitan interests and friends back to Jewish
concerns, he is called by the "sages of Sura, Pumbeditha's
wise," the scholars in the Babylonian centres where the
Talmud was compiled, and he turns to Johanan ben-
Zakkai, who founded the centre of learning at Jabna when
the Romans destroyed the Jewish commonwealth and dis-
persed the Jews. Very frequently in his poems Klein attests
not only to his knowledge of Judaism, but to his love for
these builders of Jewish scholarship.

> I followed them, I loved them, sage and saint,
> Graybeard in caftan, juggling the when and why,
> Ascetic rubbing a microscopic taint,
> Scholar on whose neat earlocks piety ascended
> In spiral to the sky—

Klein's religion was more than a nostalgic return to a
happy and secure condition of childhood, a passive acquiescence to the ways of his forefathers. His was a continuing
struggle between belief and disbelief, an attempt, not
really successful, to reconcile his ancestral faith with his
acceptance of his sceptical, contemporary society.

Despite his reverence for the great Jewish scholars and
his respect for the elaborate code of ceremony and practice
that constitutes traditional Judaism, Klein was not unaware
of the dangers of orthodoxy. In "Out of the Pulver and the
Polished Lens" (*Hath Not A Jew*) in the passage dealing
with the excommunication of Spinoza, he castigates the
rigidity of dogmatists that breeds intolerance and harsh-
ness. But such notes of condemnation are scarce in Klein's
writing and do not seriously shape his religious position.
Of much greater import are the few brief references, asides
almost, in which he confessed his own inability to hold

firmly to his faith. In "Childe Harold's Pilgrimage" (*Hath Not A Jew*) after mentioning that his forefathers gathered strength to endure historic anti-Semitism from their converse with God, he added,

> My father is gathered to his fathers, God rest his wraith!
> And his son
> Is a pauper in spirit, a beggar in piety,
> Cut off without a penny's worth of faith.

A similar and more obviously intrusive confession of doubt is to be found in a later poem, when, after describing at some length the cripples climbing on their knees the ninety-nine steps to the Oratoire de St. Joseph, the tone of ironic detachment which suggests the rationalist's sense of absurdity of the action, is dramatically broken. The poet suddenly becomes personal,

> And I who in my own faith once had faith like this,
> but have not now, am crippled more than they.

In view of such doubts co-existing with his veneration of Jewish sages and their teachings, one is tempted to apply to Klein the very comment he made about his good friend and fellow-poet, A. J. M. Smith: "Moreover, Smith is, albeit in no orthodox sense, of a 'true-religious heart'; like a Renaissance Pope, he may or may not believe in God; but all His saints he venerates." (*The Canadian Forum*, Feb., 1944, pp. 257-8).

But such a view, while undoubtedly true at times, is inadequate. Much more often than such direct assertions of disbelief are the statements which firmly express faith, the readiness to go beyond the reach of his intelligence and the limits of the self. In the poem "In Re Solomon Warshawer" (*Poems*) Klein indicates the need to overcome one's own spiritual shortcoming. In this poem, based on legend, the exiled king Solomon, the quintessential wandering Jew, says,

> Mistake me not: I am no virtuous saint.
> But I at least waged war, for holy booty
> Against my human taint.

The outcome of these struggles in Klein's poems is usually a re-affirmation of faith. In fact, usually the struggle is not with one's own spiritual inadequacy or doubts, but rather one that takes place within the framework of belief, of over-all acceptance, and it involves the need to reconcile evident injustice and suffering with faith in God's justice and mercy. The tension in these poems develops out of this attempt. This is made clear in "Reb Levi Yitschok Talks to God" and again in "Rabbi Yom-Tob of Mayence Petitions His God" (*Poems*) where he affirms "What the Lord gives, He owes; He owes no more." But the need to understand in human terms "The how and when, the wherefore and the why" remains and hence the cry,

> Let there be light
> In the two agonies that are my eyes,
> And in the dungeon of my heart, a door
> Unbarred. Descend, O Lord, and speak.

It might be argued that in these poems since the poet puts the affirmation into the mouth of his historical characters, he might simply be indicating his awareness of such responses and the strengths derived from the accepting attitude without committing himself to them. However, such statements are so frequently and sympathetically presented that it is fairly obvious from tone and context that Klein shares them. Furthermore, in very many poems he does speak in his own voice to the same effect. The thirty-six psalms in "The Psalter of Avram Haktani" (*Poems*) in mood and thought are fundamentally religious. Psalm

II is the most direct admission of his return to his traditional religious beliefs.

> How is he changed, the scoffers say,
> This hero of an earlier day, . . .
> O Lord, in this my thirtieth year
> What clever answer shall I bear
> To those slick persons amongst whom
> I sat, but was not in their room?
> How shall I make apocalypse
> Of that which rises to my lips,
> And on my lips is smitten dumb. . . .
> Do Thou the deed, say Thou the word,
> And with Thy sacred stratagem
> Do justify my ways to them.

His last and fullest statement of the spiritual odyssey from
unquestioning faith and devotion to religious learning
through doubts and denials back to faith is found in his
novel *The Second Scroll*, where "miracle" becomes the
keyword to our understanding of events and the mysterious
intertwining of good and evil. The emergence of good out
of evil suggests a power and a design beyond human comprehension, and the series of poems constituting Gloss Hai,
the final passage in the book, express unequivocally and
joyously in the language of prayer Klein's essentially religious nature.

Although Klein's attachment to the Jewish people and
its traditional religious beliefs and practices were so deeply
rooted in him that he could probably never have entirely
escaped its influence, his views and interests did undergo
change as his widening range of activities took him beyond
the culturally self-sufficient and enclosed Jewish community. It is not surprising that the adolescent, struggling to
achieve independence under these circumstances, should
have done battle with "The wicked theologic myth," and
concocted "learned blasphemies" as he tells us in Psalm II
(*Poems*). Although Klein's emancipation began when he

left Hebrew school and attended a secular high school in Montreal, it was only a slight emancipation there as almost the only non-Jews in the large school were the teachers. The broadening process really got under way when he attended McGill and later the University of Montreal. Here Klein got to know directly members of the other two racial groups that with the Jews constituted the tripartite population of Montreal, and perhaps even more important he came to know the riches of a culture other than his native one. The impact of the great figures of English literature, Chaucer, Shakespeare, and Donne, in particular, was considerable. By the beginning of the 1930s Klein, like most young poets of the time, came under the influence of T. S. Eliot. Although for the most part Klein still dealt with Jewish experience, his style in such poems as "The Soirée of Velvel Kleinburger" and in passages even in "Reb Levi Yitschok Talks to God," reflected Eliot's. The colloquialisms, the use of refrain, the seemingly disjointed phrases, are obviously borrowed characteristics and even the poet's attitude of cynical despair, of condescending pity and humorous contempt for Kleinburger are an imitation of Eliot's treatment of Prufrock and Sweeney. Like most writers of this period Klein was stirred by the effects of the depression and then the Spanish Civil War. His radicalism at this time, a continuing political attitude—he stood for Parliament as a C.C.F. candidate in 1948—does not indicate a reversal in his basic social response, for it did not stem from a determinist or materialist philosophy, but from a moral passion nurtured by the Hebrew prophets. This increasing concern with the general issues confronting society was reflected in such poems as "Barricade Smith, His Speeches," "Blueprint for a Monument of War," and "Of Castles in Spain," none of which he saw fit to re-publish when his collections of poems appeared. His association with the emerging group of able young Montreal poets, particularly A. J. M. Smith and F. R. Scott, became closer. Together with Leo Kennedy, Robert Finch and E.

J. Pratt, they constituted the distinctive group whose work was published in *New Provinces*, 1936. Two related forces, however, Zionism and anti-Semitism, both significant elements in the Jewish tradition, kept Klein from drifting far from his Jewish concerns; in fact, they intensified his commitment to his heritage.

In 1927 while still a student at McGill, Klein became president of Canadian Young Judaea, a national Zionist youth organization. Shortly after, he became editor of its paper, *The Judaean*. His involvement in Jewish affairs deepened when he was appointed assistant executive director of the Zionist Organization of Canada, directed its educational programme, and in 1936 edited *The Canadian Zionist*. He became a regular contributor to the *Canadian Jewish Chronicle* and in 1939 assumed the editorship of this Anglo-Jewish paper in Montreal, a position which he held until 1955. In these posts he became one of the outstanding leaders and probably the most effective spokesman for the Canadian Jewish community. The effort to establish a Jewish Homeland in Palestine and the need to expose and combat anti-Semitism became his daily burden.

Klein's intensified preoccupation with Jewish issues in the late 1930s and 1940s is reflected in the fact that he chose for his first volume of poetry, *Hath Not A Jew* (1940), only poems dealing with Jewish matters. He deals with Jewish legend and history, the struggle to realize the dream of nationhood in Palestine, and he rejoices in the variety of Jewish characters and activities. Even when he might have been critical he refrained, his deft ironic humour, as we see in such poems as "Landlord," "Shadchon," and "Preacher," softening comments that might otherwise have been caustic. In part this attitude reflects Klein's broad tolerance, a comprehensive affection for all mankind, except the haters, which reminds one of Chaucer. In part, however, he might have refrained because this book is in some sense an apologia, a conscious defence of his people, as the very title of the book suggests. Although in the opening poem "Ave Atque Vale" the apolgia has in it a tinge of apology, for the most part the portraits that Klein presents are a proud display of his heritage, a dignified counter-portrait to the degrading image projected by the Nazis. One of the most frequently recurring themes is that of anti-Semitism, a theme that Klein examines from many aspects and to which he responds in many moods.

The poems that deal with anti-Semitism in Klein's first volume taken together reveal through their themes, imagery and allusions, a many-sided and rather full consideration of the problem. Whether they were consciously selected for this purpose or not is hard to say, but certainly they reveal how the mind of the poet grappled with the issue. Although this theme was given terrible and immediate significance by the German Nazis and their imitators, Klein, drawing on a great deal of knowledge, historical and contemporary, gives the topic a perspective needed for adequate understanding. In "Childe Harold's Pilgrimage" Klein depicts the contemporary scene in which the western nations remained relatively indifferent to the catastrophe overwhelming the Jews, equivocating and delaying their deliberations on refugees, and for the most part refusing them admission. The emphasis in this poem is on the Nazi outrage which Klein castigates in staccato, ironic phrases, and in a tone of fierce mockery that foreshadows *The Hitleriad*. The next poem in this volume dealing with hostility to the Jews, "Sonnet in Time of Affliction," through its allusions to David, Bar Cochba and the Maccabees, touches on three different periods in Jewish history when the people were endangered by the Philistines, Romans, and Hellenized Syrians. In a series of poems that follows, "Design for Mediaeval Tapestry," Klein treats of the Christian persecution of the Jews in the Middle Ages.

Klein not only makes reference to varying moments in history to establish a context for the contemporary phenomenon of anti-Semitism; he also explores in these poems the various ways in which it manifests itself and the varying motives behind it. In "Childe Harold's Pilgrimage" Nazi anti-Semitism is seen as an insensate, primitive racial rage, violent and sadistic. In "Design for Mediaeval Tapestry" the basic motive was religious antagonism supplemented by greedy desire for material and sexual plunder. And in the last poem in this volume on this subject, Poem V of "Sonnets Semitic," Klein returns to the modern period, but the aspect of anti-Semitism presented differs from the others: here Klein reveals the polite prejudice which does not destroy but merely limits and humiliates.

Klein was at least as much concerned with the nature of the Jewish response to this external threat. The twentieth-century speaker in "Childe Harold's Pilgrimage" considers and rejects prayer, though he recognizes the strength his forefathers derived from it under similar circumstances, because he is cut off from his faith. He rejects Esau's argument because violence is antithetical to the traditional way of life developed by the ghetto Jew, and he does not accept the escape offered by suicide, for such an ignoble end is a denial of the worth and dignity of one's heritage. The only defence the poet here envisages is

> The frozen patience waiting for its day,
> The stance long-suffering, the stoic word,
> The bright empirics that knows well that the
> Night of the Cauchemar comes and goes away,—

In the eleven poems that constitute "Design for Mediaeval Tapestry" Klein depicts a wider range of responses: attempts to escape through flight, fearful hiding or apostasy; and varying attitudes that prompt acceptance. Some, as Klein points out, accept their condition passively, displaying a fatalistic resignation ("Reb Daniel Shochet reflects")—or acquiescence in the will of God ("Nahum-

this-is-also-for-the-good ponders"). Others, accepting also
like Nahum the justice of God's acts, postulate their own
guilty, sinful nature, and attempt to persuade Him to
change His will through their repentance and reform. Still
others, however, refuse to escape or acquiesce. In "Job
reviles" God is arraigned for his failure to act, while in the
last poem in this series, "Esther hears echoes of his voice,"
there is a passionate demand for an explanation.

In *Poems* (1944) Klein is less preoccupied by the theme
of anti-Semitism. Psalm VI is a moving total indictment
of mankind for the Nazi horrors, perpetrated or tolerated,
and Psalm XXV simply asks for an explanation of "the
folded present." In two long poems in this volume, "In Re
Solomon Warshawer" and "Rabbi Yom-Tob of Mayence
Petitions His God," Klein does, however, restate aspects
of this theme developed in his earlier volume. In *The
Hitleriad* (1944), a thematically simple and direct satire,
Klein catalogues the Nazis and their crimes. Despite the
explosive force of Klein's wrath in this poem, and the
sharpness of his wit, the poem fails primarily because no
amount of rhetorical sarcastic sneers and name-calling, no
collection of insults or invective, it matters not how effectively phrased—and some lines are very effective—can
convey adequately the shock that came from the recognition of the possible extent of human depravity.

With the cessation of the war and the defeat of Nazi
Germany, the threat of anti-Semitism waned and Klein's
poetic interest in the subject ceased. It was a crucial theme
for him not merely because he felt that he and his people
were threatened, but because this complex and pervasive
phenomenon with its social and religious implications
revealed much about the nature of man and his inter-
relationships with his fellow men and with God. In so
far as it raised the question of evil and God's relation to it,
this theme impinged directly on Klein's religious ideas,
tested his belief. The fullest exploration of this aspect of
this theme is to be found in the novel *The Second Scroll*.

The problem of anti-Semitism related also to Klein's commitment to the Zionist cause. He welcomed the restoration of the spirit of independence and self-reliance that the Zionist effort brought to the Jews in their confrontation with anti-Semitism. But Zionism was a much more meaningful concept than merely a mechanism for self-defence or even for the realization of a nationalist objective. If anti-Semitism was the negative agent, the centripetal force compelling Klein to the centre of Jewish experience, Zionism was the positive force attracting and holding him there with a religious fervour. Franz Kafka, in a reflection, commented that the Zionists had grabbed hold of an edge of the "tallith" (prayer shawl) as it disappeared around the corner in the twentieth century. This shrewd observation, made long before its truth was as obvious as it is today, applies only in small measure to Klein, for to him the nationalist ideal never became a substitute for the religious one. For Klein, the reach for Zion, was, as it had always been traditionally, a religious yearning. Zion had an imaginative reality and expressed an imaginative and spiritual need, like the world of his childhood which he sought to regain in memory.

> It is a fabled city that I seek;
> It stands in Space's vapours and Time's haze.

("Autobiographical," Gloss Aleph, *The Second Scroll*)

The nationalist impulse, which Klein also fully accepted, was but an expression of the urge for redemption and an attempt in twentieth-century terms to realize it. Though Klein may have had misgivings about other aspects of Judaism, in this issue he never wavered.

Klein's involvement in Zionist activity began early. In the late 1920s and 1930s he was active in Canadian Young Judaea, and later in the Zionist Organization of Canada. This interest in Zionism was reflected early in his poetry. In January 1930, at the age of 21, he published in *The*

Menorah Journal (later reprinted in *Hath Not A Jew*) a sequence of poems "Greeting on This Day" in which he considers various aspects of Zionism, the terror and the wonder of the new life in the Holy Land, the relationship of Jew to Arab, the development of the new Jewish prototype, the straight-backed pioneer Jew. These two themes are reiterated in two other "Zionist" poems in *Hath Not A Jew*, "Sonnet in Time of Affliction" and Poem II, "Sonnets Semitic." In the former Klein is distressed by the violence that compels those who seek to rebuild peacefully the Homeland to answer with force. The second poem, whose opening line is an echo of the last line of "Sonnet in Time of Affliction," emphasizes with its imagery of white doves and orange blossoms the joyful aspect of the return to Zion. In "Yehuda Ha-Levi, His Pilgrimage" (*Poems*), a long allegorical romance about the exile of the Jewish people from their Homeland and attempted return by the poet-philosopher Yehuda Ha-Levi, Klein reveals clearly his own passionate longing for the return. The fullest statement of Klein's Zionist concept is to be found in his novel, *The Second Scroll*, where the national theme is most clearly interwoven with the religious theme, for the search for Zion is inseparable from the search for God and an understanding of His ways; its attainment is seen as a miraculous manifestation of His will.

Though Klein was shaped by his beginnings and then impelled by the forces of the 1930s and 1940s to concern himself primarily with the experiences of the Jewish people, this concentration of interest did not diminish his achievement. As E. K. Brown has pointed out, the effect has been enlarging rather than limiting, for Klein's world of characters, events and ideas possesses "a solidity and an intensity . . . very rare in our literature." Although Klein drew considerably on his heritage, his poems usually depict human traits that are universal and express a religious or moral attitude common to Christian and Jew. E. J. Pratt, in a review of *The Hitleriad* (*Canadian Forum*, Oct. 1944) stated that "Despite the difficulties springing out of his scholasticism, his legalistic lore, and his Talmudic terms and references which needed footnotes, Klein could appeal to us on the basis of a moral culture common to Jew and Gentile—that of the Hebrew prophet and psalmist. All of his best work possessed this appeal, whether it was the ringing affirmation of Isaiah or the subdued litanies of Jeremiah, Ecclesiastes, and David."

Klein's interests were not merely Jewish. Canada, too, was part of his heritage. In the 1930s, as has been briefly noted, he was closely associated with the *New Provinces* poetry group, affected by the literary influences of Eliot and the seventeenth-century metaphysicals, and by such social conditions as the depression and the rise of fascism. In the early 1940s he was part of a group of active Montreal poets, which included Patrick Anderson and Irving Layton, who published in *Preview* and *First Statement*, the forerunner of *Northern Review*. Partly as a result of the impetus of this new poetic movement, and in part reflecting the intensifying sense of Canadian nationalism widely felt at the end of World War II, Klein felt drawn to the Canadian scene generally. With the defeat of Hitler and the removal of the menace of anti-Semitism, Klein's imagination was less dominated by the Jewish condition and he felt released from his burden of responsibility as Jewish spokesman. He no longer needed to cry his outcry, or to set beside the ugly stereotyped portrait of the Jew, the Jew and his tradition as he knew them. In *The Rocking Chair and Other Poems* (1948) Klein turned to new themes.

The subjects of the poems in this last volume are taken for the most part from the city and the province in which Klein lived. They are perceptive and sympathetic commentaries on people and the objects and activities which express essential aspects of their lives. Generally speaking, however, the poet is less personally involved in his material than in his earlier poems. His tone is quieter, less declamatory and less urgent. He achieves greater objectivity and even greater artistic control because he maintains a measure of detachment from his subject. In his earlier poems the poet wrote from within the world he depicted, totally committed to it, expressed warmly, with a sense of immediacy and intimacy, its achievements and dreams, its pride and its fears. Despite the dangers which such psychological proximity and commitment pose for the artist—excessive emotionalism, and the subordination of artistic and critical considerations to extra-literary concerns—weaknesses from which Klein was not entirely free, these poems speak directly and forcefully to us. The poems in *The Rocking Chair and Other Poems* are much more controlled, the poet no doubt finding it easier to order his feelings and to shape his expression of them when dealing with grain elevators or frigidaires, or even when describing Mount Royal or Monsieur Gaston.

While contrasts between Klein's last poems and his earlier ones can easily be drawn, both groups reflect certain continuing characteristics of the poet. Klein still searches for the archetypal image to sum up an aspect of a society or a culture, a symbol of a condition or tradition whether it be a shrine, a rocking chair or oxen "lyric with horns," banks or pawnbrokers, liquor stores or filling stations. His sensitivity to tradition makes him the readier to discover those symbols which aptly distinguish a people. Delicately and accurately Klein depicts phases of French-Canadian life—their sustaining faith, the demagoguery of the politicians, the emphasis on class in a hierarchical order. In the title poem, "The Rocking Chair," Klein successfully conveys the mood and pace of French-Canadian life, its slow conservatism. Though for the most part Klein refrains from comment, through his use of irony the poet shows that he is not unaware of shortcomings. He has always, however, a sympathetic understanding, even an affection, for the Canadien. Deeply rooted himself in an old tradition, he responds sensitively to the French-Canadian tradition. In an article which appeared in *Les Gants du Ciel*, Dr. A. J. M. Smith, underlined this relationship. "Dans l'entité patriarcale, traditionelle et ecclésiastique qu'est le Canada francais, Klein a trouvé un univers que sa sensibilité juive lui permet de comprendre et d'aimer."

Klein's traditionalism, his conscious attempt to re-create the Jewish world past and present as he experienced it in all its particularity, affected his style and language. The influence of Biblical rhythms with its balanced and contrapuntal effects is obvious in many of Klein's poems, but the effect on his language is even more notable. Clearly, in part, Klein's language is distinctive because he, the poet, is unique, with his own "flavour" and outlook, his own tastes. But his diction is distinctive also because the world he describes is unique and he wished to convey this quality. Klein, though born in Canada, belongs to that generation of Jews that came from Europe, and fashioned for itself its own community in Canada quite separate and almost complete. This community developed its own character and personality within the national pattern, a part of the prevailing Canadian mosaic. Through the special qualities of his language, the use of foreign words, especially Hebraic and uncommon English words, and his imagery with its exotic and at times esoteric qualities, Klein tried to achieve a kind of linguistic apartness that would reinforce the similar impression of the community and its traditions that he was writing about. Words and phrases like "malefic djinns," "cognomened," "alembic," "cauchemar," "shadchan" and "pilpul trick," appear frequently. His poetry is filled with allusions to the Bible and post-Biblical Jewish sources, often relatively unknown, and much of his imagery is drawn from the same sources and from religious ceremony and ritual. The sky on Passover night "is dotted like th'unleavened bread" and the moon is a golden seder platter used for the Passover Feast (Haggadah). In speaking of the poet Yehuda Ha-Levi on

his journey to the Holy Land, Klein invokes rich images
associated with the place.

> And from the beaker of the soul, that wine
> Which sours not; and from the bowled brain
> Grape clusters torn from paradisal vine;
> Honey of Samson's bees; and milk from Pharaoh's kine!

We find the same linguistic tendency when he writes about
the French-Canadian community in *The Rocking Chair
and Other Poems*. The scholarly librarian, Monsieur
Delorme, is described as one who so loves bindings and the
old régime "that in his mind is gobelin'd fleur de lys." The
description of Montreal not only conveys its history
through image and allusion, but its character through the
Gallicized vocabulary.

> Grand port of navigations, multiple
> The lexicons uncargo'd at your quays,
> Sonnant though strange to me; but chiefest, I,
> Auditor of your music, cherish the
> Joined double-melodied vocabulaire
> Where English vocable and roll Ecossic,
> Mollified by the parle of French
> Bilinguefact your air!

Although Klein in this poem carries this device to such an
extent that the poem becomes almost a linguistic tour de
force, the result, on the whole, is startlingly effective.

Klein's traditionalism, then, shaped and directed his
creative powers. It provided him with a body of experience
from the living past that stirred his imagination and his
feelings, and at the same time enabled him to consider
contemporary events in historical perspective, a capacity
which gave depth and added meaning to his experiences.
His source of inspiration was the Jewish tradition and he
remained fixed, rooted, in its schemes of reference and
moral values, but the arc of his angle of vision widened so
that he embraced much more.

The Polished Lens: Poetic Techniques of Pratt and Klein

Dorothy Livesay

In this essay, which appeared in Canadian Literature *No. 25, Dorothy Livesay compares the poetic resources of the two leading Canadian poets of the Thirties and Forties, and finds Pratt wanting. It is reprinted by permission of the author.*

Dorothy Livesay is, with Louis Dudek, Margaret Avison, A. J. M. Smith and Irving Layton, one of Klein's contemporaries and colleagues in the development of a "modernist" Canadian poetry. Her first collection was The Green Pitcher *(1928) and her most recent books are* The Unquiet Bed *(1967),* The Documentaries *(1968) and* Plainsong *(1969).*

The style is the Man. That familiar saying recalls what T. S. Eliot stressed in his analysis of Ezra Pound's poetry:

People may think they like the form because they like the content, or they think they like the content because they like the form. In the perfect poet they fit and are the same thing; and in another sense they are always the same thing.

A study, therefore, of the styles of two Canadian poets can be useful only if it delivers into our minds a clearer understanding of the poet's approach to his work, his themes. My aim here is not an analysis of technique for its own sake, but of technique for the sake of enlightenment.

In retrospect, the language of our Post-Confederation poets is singularly conventional and dull. Though often felicitous in its music and imagery it swings, supine, in a

hammock: "'golden and inappellable".[1] Adjectives pre-
dominate over verbs; and even such a good imagist as
Lampman pads out his lines with useless words, simply to
fit the required metre. In these poets there is no sense of
being "seized" by language, in the Joycean way. By 1920
it was clear there was a crying need to liberate the language of poetry in Canada; and an equally urgent need to
turn from the contemplation of nature to concern for the
human condition.

The first sign of experimentation in both areas came
with the publication of *Newfoundland Verse* by E. J.
Pratt, in 1923; and more markedly with his *Titans,* 1926.
Pratt, a robust talker from our northeastern shore, set
Toronto crackling with his "Cachalot" and "Witches'
Brew." The language was fresh, muscular, contemporary
and often boisterously amusing. The metre was one that
had been rarely practised by a Canadian poet: octosyllabic
couplets with an anapaestic roll, "perched on a dead
volcanic pile"; and the content was not too strenuous to
tax the average man's ingenuity. It bore with it strong
echoes of mock heroic epic and light satire. Like Pope or
Dryden, Pratt did not distrust the world he mocked, nor
did he wish to destroy it. He felt it could stand up to
attack. The style of these early extravaganzas, accordingly,
was marked by punch and zest, the metre moving at a run
or a gallop by means of strong, monosyllabic verbs; the
rhyme staccato, to punctuate the humour.

> They ate and drank and fought, it's true,
> And when the zest was on they slew;
> And yet their most tempestuous quarrels
> Were never prejudiced by morals.
>   ("The Witches' Brew")

With his next poem, "The Great Feud," it would seem
from the style alone that Pratt had begun to be aware of

[1] D. C. Scott, "The Height of Land," in *Selected Poems* (Toronto:
Ryerson, 1951).

some conflict in his position. As Desmond Pacey has pointed out, "Passages of horrible conflict alternate with passages of rollicking humour." The theme is a more serious one than that of the "Cachalot" or "The Witches' Brew"; and yet the poet relies on the same octosyllabics, enjambment and witty rhyme to carry the rhythm of the fable. Agreed, the myth-making, story-telling elements are Pratt's own; but he does not support these with imagery, epithet, or colour. His chief structural weakness on the syntactic level (to be explored more fully later) is already evident. Pratt depends too fully on the prepositional phrase. On one page of 28 lines, chosen at random, there are 24 phrases: endless lists of nouns. Variety is gained, notwithstanding, by means of ingenuity in the choice of vocabulary and end-rhymes.

If we now compare Abraham Klein's earliest work with Pratt's *phase one* we find that his technical power, evident at the age of twenty, was amazingly versatile. Of the two poets Milton Wilson has remarked, justly, that at this period "Their diction often calls for the same critical adjectives: polysyllabic, technical, erudite, as well as colloquial or prosaic," and in metre and rhyme Klein might be thought to be echoing if not imitating the older poet. Yet already in his first book, *Hath Not A Jew* (1940), Klein appears to have at his command a dazzling variety of poetic forms. The verse (never "free" and rarely unrhymed) ranges widely through octosyllabics, heroic couplets, *terza rima*; and from short bursts of lyricism to the long, sinuous biblical line with its caesura and parallelism:

> If this be a Jew, indeed, where is the crook of his spine;
> and the quiver of his lip, where?
> Behold his knees are not callous through kneeling; he
> is proud, he is erect.
>
> ("Greeting on this Day")

The effect here is created by the use of caesura or *juncture*, as it is now commonly called by prosodists. Besides the normal juncture between words Klein indicates, in Line One by means of punctuation, a pause accompanied by a rise in pitch which serves to place added stress and interest on the second rhetorical sentence:

If this be a Jew—indeed/where is the crook of his spine—

In Line Two, the placing of the rising juncture stresses the question word, "where":

        and the quiver of his lip/where—

In the next line the choice of the rhetorical word "behold" in itself creates a dramatic juncture:

Behold | his knees are not callous through kneeling—he—
        is proud | he is erect—

It is by means of such skilful techniques as this that Klein creates his powerful rhythms. Klein uses rhyme also to emphasize his metrical effects. He has a notable facility with rhyme; and in his work it is difficult to find a rhyme that does not sound natural, at home. In the tetrameter stanzas he explores many variations in rhyme scheme and in the *terza rima* he varies one-syllabled with two-syllabled rhymes so that the rhythm is constantly subject to a new charge:

> Seek reasons; rifle your theology;
> Philosophize; expand your dialectic;
> Decipher and translate God's diary;
>
> Discover causes, primal and eclectic;
> I cannot; all I know is this:
> That pain doth render flesh most sore and hectic;
>
> That lance-points prick; that scorched bones hiss;
> That thumb-screws agonize, and that a martyr
> Is mad if he considers these things bliss.
>   ("Design for Mediæval Tapestry")

In this book, *Hath Not A Jew*, Klein established himself as a master of the craft. Added to the singular felicity of his metre and rhyme was the delight in vocabulary and the contrapuntal use of pause, or juncture, as evident in the poem quoted above (particularly effective in the last two verses and helpfully marked by semi-colons and colon).

On now, to *phase two*, where Pratt's development will again be parallelled with Klein's. Pratt's work of interest here is *The Titanic* (1935), a poem in which he extricates himself from the tetrametric clutch. His line is extended now to heroic couplets. These, at their lowest level, can be platitudinous and dull:

> Her intercostal spaces ready to start
> The power pulsing through her lungs and heart
> An ocean lifeboat in herself, so ran
> The architectural comment on her plan.

At the highest level, where the rhymes are more freely arranged, the features of enjambment and juncture create an inner tension which is most pleasing:

> Pressure and glacial time had stratified
> The berg to the consistency of flint,
> And kept inviolate, through clash of tide,
> And gale, façade and columns with their hint
> Of inward altars and of steeple bells
> Ringing the passage of the parallels.

These images are common ones, more vividly played upon by Melville ("The Berg") and by Roberts ("The Iceberg"); but Pratt's vocabulary saves the day, with quite a brilliant display of tension between polysyllabic words of classical origin (*consistency, inviolate, parallels*) and a catalogue of single-syllabled nouns: *gale, hint, bells, berg, flint, clash, tide*.

It must be faced however: Pratt's passion for nouns leads him into two serious difficulties. One is the absence of texture; for without adjectives and adverbs it is not easy to appeal to the senses. And where, in Pratt's poetry, is there any evocation of touch, taste, hearing, scent? True, the visual appeal is there: "sloping spur that tapered to a claw"; but this is an appeal in outline, in black and white. One senses that the poet is colour-blind. The adjectives which he does use, sparingly, call no colours into view: *lateral, casual, polar, eternal, southern, glacial.*

But the monotony of Pratt's verse can be traced, I believe, to a deeper, structural cause. Because he is so concerned with "naming"—adding up nouns—he must catch hold of them by using two devices: by cataloguing; or by dangling them from the hooks of prepositions. It is rarely possible to find a line of Pratt without a prepositional phrase; more often there are two or three bolstering it up. In the lines quoted above this pattern can be seen in five of the six. In the second line there are two prepositional phrases; in the third, two; in the fourth, two.

Now this pattern, in itself, is not deplorable: it is an essential element in English syntax. Praise of the noun (sometimes amounting to adoration!) can be found in much contemporary critical and creative writing. Gertrude Stein puts it one way:

Poetry is concerned with using with abusing with losing and wanting, with denying with avoiding with adoring with replacing the noun. . . . Poetry is doing nothing but using refusing and pleasing and betraying and caressing nouns.[2]

and here is Harry R. Warfel, a linguist:

But how do these nouns come to be used so much? They play as subjects of verbs, as complements of verbs and verbals, as objects of prepositions, as independent elements, as headwords. What is important is their mode of turning up everywhere. For example, nearly every noun can be the object of several prepositions. If the working

[2]Gertrude Stein, "What is Poetry"; in *The Language of Wisdom and Folly*, edited by Irving J. Lee. Harper, 1949.

vocabulary of English has 200,000 nouns and these unite
with only an average of ten prepositions, the result is two
million adjective and/or adverb phrases. If you have ever
wondered why some writers clutter their style with prepositional phrases, you can now see why.[3]

A skilful poet then, writing in English, will certainly use
nouns to his advantage to vary the stress and juncture;
but Pratt, I feel, tends to use nouns to his disadvantage.
For instance, the indiscriminate use of "of" followed by
nouns (lines 5 and 6) ends, from sheer repetition, in
rhythmic paralysis.

As we have seen, Klein's metrical range was wider at the
start than was Pratt's. In his *phase two* Klein continued to
employ polysyllabics as well as the heroic couplet. Understandably therefore in *The Hitleriad* (1944) there are
echoes of Pratt's style. The form is not narrative like "The
Great Feud" but the intention is equally satiric:

And then there came,—blow, trumpets; drummers, drum
The apocalypse, the pandemonium
The war the Kaiser from his shrivelled hand
Let fall upon the European land

Noticeable even in this unremarkable stanza is the use of
juncture for dramatic effect; of finite verbs; of inversion;
and of clausal patterns which create rhythmic variation.
Further on Klein writes:

Club-footed, rat-faced, halitotic, the
Brave Nordic ideal, a contrario!
A kept man; eloquent, a Ph.D;
Carried no gun, forsooth; a radio
Lethal enough for him, shouting its lies
Exploding lebensraum and libido;
Subtle in puncturing all human foibles
Saving his own, prolific in alibis—
Goebbels.

---

[3] Harry R. Warfel, "Structural Linguistics and Composition" in *College
English*, Vol. 20, 1958-59.

The Hitleriad is not a successful poem. It lacks an element which Pratt possessed in good measure: objectivity. Nonetheless as a long poem it is interesting to compare with one of Pratt's because, technically, it rings many more changes. Thereby it achieves pace; and on another level, irony.

In the same year, 1944, Klein's real lyricism burst forth in his "psalms," thirty-six short poems in a great variety of forms (published in *Poems*). Several are closely patterned on the Psalms of David in their long lines, parallelism, Hebrew inversions and rhetoric. Others leap away from anything but a superficial resemblance to the English iambic pentameter and allow strong stress rhythm, reminiscent of Anglo-Saxon and of Hebrew, to take over. Here is a delightful example, from Psalm XXVII, "a psalm to teach humility":

> O sign and wonder of the barnyard, more
> beautiful than the pheasant, more melodious
> than nightingale! O creature marvellous!
>
> Prophet of sunrise, and foreteller of times!
> Vizier of the constellations! Sage,
> red-bearded, scarlet turbaned, in whose brain
> the stars lie scattered like well-scattered grain!
> Calligraphist upon the barnyard page!
> Five-noted balladist! Crower of rhymes!

But this is Klein in his gayest, tenderest mood. He can be more easily likened to Pratt in a poem called "In Re Solomon Warshawer." Pratt's "The Truant" is quite comparable because it represents Pratt at a high technical level, breaking away from the confines of rigid metre. The heroic couplet still holds the thought in check, but in "The Truant" it is loosened, stretched or abbreviated to avoid monotony. The tone is vigorous, satiric; and the theme is man himself, pitted against a mechanical universe.

Sire

The stuff is not amenable to fire
There still remains that strange precipitate
Which has the quality to resist
Our oldest and most trusted catalyst

Lines such as these retain Pratt's robust, semi-scientific vocabulary; and his wit takes up the slack caused by the obsessive use of prepositional phrases. I find this Pratt's most interesting poem, both for its technical virtuosity and for its provocative thought. Man is being judged: but he reverses the tables, himself condemning "God" for creating a purely mechanical universe. In Klein's "In Re Solomon Warshawer" there also occurs a judgment scene; in this case between the evil forces in man, and the good. Man's plea before the court (a wartime tribunal) is that of the underdog, of the one in process of being destroyed, the Jew. The abstract Jew however is so particularized that the reader is constrained to identify with him (as also is the case in "The Truant").

Here is a Nazi soldier reporting to his superior:

Asked for his papers, he made a great to-do
of going through the holes in his rags, whence he withdrew
a Hebrew pamphlet and a signet ring,
herewith produced, exhibits 1 and 2.

I said, No document in a civilized tongue?
He replied:

Produce, O Lord, my wretched finger print,
Bring forth, O angel in the heavenly court,
My dossier, full, detailed, both fact and hint,
Felony, misdemeanor, tort!

I refused to be impressed by talk of that sort.

But passionate identification with the rightness of man's cause heightens the language to a degree not found in "The Truant." Consider the lines which begin

> They would have harried me extinct, those thrones.
> Set me, archaic, in their heraldries,
> Blazon antique! . . .

Rhyme is forgotten. Iambic regularity is broken by strong stresses aided by trochaic and dactyllic rhythms. Added to these features are those of inversion, juncture, and punctuation used for intonational effect. In this respect the entire poem is a forerunner of poems in *The Rocking Chair* (1948) where:

> it is tradition. Centuries have flicked
> from its arcs, alternately flicked and pinned.
> It rolls with the gait of St. Malo. It is act
> and symbol, symbol of this static folk.

Here, most cunningly within the apparent framework of the iambic pentameter, Klein has overlaid the four-stress beat of much Hebrew poetry and caught at the same time the lilt of the French language. He achieves this *tour de force*, I believe, by emphasizing the four levels of stress; distinguishing between syllables that are nearly neutral and thus "outriders" in Hopkins' sense (alternately) and those that bear tertiary, secondary or primary stress. His use of juncture aids in this process also, as it is always well-timed (or isochronic).

By the time Klein's *Rocking Chair* appeared Pratt was already well established in his phase three, with *Brebeuf and his Brethren,* a long documentary narrative based on Quebec's history and religious past. The epic length and scope of this poem would indicate that Pratt conceived it as a major production. But surely it could be criticized as a conventional piece rather than a creative one, for in form and intention it is eminently Victorian! Nor is it comparable with the later experimental poetry of Klein. On the technical level both poets have thrown off their patterned style, have pushed rhyme into the background, have sought a free flowing rhythm close to the rhythm of speech. But what speech? I would dare to say that Pratt's speech here is prosaic, generalized; whereas Klein's has the vernacular lilt, and is particular.

In *Brébeuf* Pratt offers us a steady but not a heady blank verse. Would not the opening lines, apparently attempting to create atmosphere, be equally effective if written as prose? And the second stanza is surely one long, wordy list, noun following upon noun?

> The story of a frontier like a saga
> Rang through the cells and cloisters of a nation.

This is not to say that *Brébeuf* is not without its moments of poetic intensity. In Stanza XII particularly the iambic line is made undulant and ominous by means of dactyllic and falling rhythms. Then the poem climbs again to the climax, a simple image of

> In the sound of invisible trumpets blowing
> Around two slabs of board, right-angled, hammered
> By Roman nails and hung on a Jewish hill. . . .

These are the heights; but there are too many valleys where vocabulary, syntax, rhythm and imagery reveal only mediocrity.

How different has been the development of Abraham Klein! Behind him lies the shadow of three languages, three traditions. The Jewish writer in Montreal can indeed be said to bridge the English and French cultures, and to inject into these languages the rhythms, inversions, pauses and parallelisms peculiar to Hebrew and Yiddish.

> Then he will remember his travels over that body—
> the torso verb, the beautiful face of the noun,
> and all those shaped and warm auxiliaries!
> A first love it was, the recognition of his own.
> Dear limbs adverbial, complexion of adjective,
> dimple and dip of conjugation!
>   ("Portrait of the Poet as Landscape")

In those lines of Klein we find the contemporaneous sound of the "loosened" iambic employed by Spender, Auden, Day Lewis, where the strong stresses pull the lines up short and leave words like "auxiliaries," "recognition" and "conjugation" with only one strong stress. We find also the emotional, rhetorical lilt of the Hebrew, created by inversion ("Dear limbs adverbial"), by dactyls, and then the counterpoint rhythm that surely echoes the French. This note sounds clearly in short poems such as "Political Meeting".

> he is their idol: like themselves, not handsome,
> not snobbish, not of the *Grande Allée. Un homme!*

and also in that marvellous linguistic carnival: "Montreal." In his linguistic sensitivity Klein is a surpassing fine juggler, holding three globes in his hand and tossing them about with dazzling dexterity. In this no other Canadian poet is his equal.

Let me now set down my hope that this examination of the style of two poets has revealed something of their attitude as creators. For me, Pratt is a self-made poet; Klein, a natural one, possessing a Blakeian simplicity. Pratt remained a story-teller to the end, an "old artificer" collecting artifacts and arranging them cunningly, without committing his deeper self. The man, like the style, is easily identified. As W. E. Collin has noted, "his mind has undergone a scholar's discipline, it never runs berserk." Klein, a scholar also but in a narrower discipline, probed inwards to the human soul, revealing its possibilities for creative joy as well as its predilections for darkness, madness.

> Palsy the keeper of the house;
> And of strongmen take Thy toll.
> Break down the twigs; break down the boughs,
> But touch not, Lord, the golden bowl!

(from Psalm XXII: "A prayer for Abraham, against madness.")

Abraham Klein and the Problem of Synthesis

John Matthews

This article appeared in the first number of the Journal of Commonwealth Literature *(University of Leeds, Sept. 1965). It is reprinted by permission of the author and Heinemann Educational Books Ltd.*

John Matthews is a professor of English at Queen's University. Author of Tradition in Exile, *a comparative study of Canadian and Australian literature in the nineteenth century, Professor Matthews was the first Director of the inter-disciplinary Institute for Commonwealth and Comparative Studies at Queen's. He is concerned here to demonstrate that* The Second Scroll *unifies and "imposes a clear pattern" on the work of Klein's earlier periods.*

Abraham Moses Klein was born in Montreal in 1909, the son of a poor potter who was a strictly orthodox member of the Jewish faith. M. W. Steinberg has remarked that Montreal was "one of the most intensely Jewish communities in North America," but one must also keep in mind the relationship of Klein's minority group to others in his native city, and its relation to the rest of Canada. Perhaps nowhere more clearly than in Montreal is the relationship between minorities and majorities more complex, or more indicative of the general Canadian tendency to choose the mosaic rather than the melting pot. At the time of Klein's birth the Jewish minority was enclosed within an English-speaking minority in a French-speaking city and province which was itself a minority in terms of the whole country—a bewildering series of Chinese boxes. While it was to be many years before the full implications of this complex were to appear in Klein's work, they were a vital part of the background which produced him.

Young Klein went to schools in Montreal, learning in a pious home the rudiments of Hebrew religion and in public school, as he has said, "the rudiments of arithmetic and race prejudice."[1] Yet he goes on to say that his childhood was a particularly happy one, and he came to know racial discrimination less obviously and less painfully than would have been the case in many other countries.[2] Intellectually precocious, he absorbed much Jewish history and philosophy; at this time his greatest ambition was to become a rabbi. Instead, by winning scholarships he graduated in Arts from McGill University, where the language of instruction was English, and went on to the French-speaking Université de Montréal to study law before being admitted to the Quebec bar in 1933.

The reasons that he gave for this resolute bi-culturalism (or perhaps tri-culturalism) are recounted by Father Régimbal in his article "Les Artistes israèlites au Canada francais." Quoting a conversation with Klein, he says:

M. Klein choisit délibérément de faire ses études en droit en français à l'Université de Montréal. 'J'avais conscience alors', dit-il, 'de prendre contact avec une culture dont la discipline intellectuelle et la pensée même s'apparentaient à ma formation première, de tradition talmudique.'[3]

Reared in a communal group which fiercely preserved its own intellectual and moral discipline as the core of its continuing identity, Klein was convinced that a man must find his tradition of ethical absolutes and stand squarely within it. His university education gave him the opportunity of examining the equivalents in the English and French communities.

During his years at university Klein published verse, not only in college magazines, but in *Canadian Forum* (1931 et seq.), *Poetry* (1929 et seq.), and regularly in the

---

[1] Quoted by Louis Dudek, *Canadian Forum*, XXX, 11.
[2] *Saturday Night*, LXV, 12, 46.
[3] *Relations*, VIII (June 1948), 184-5.

Jewish weekly *Menorah Journal.* In 1933 he began to practise law in Montreal, and became a principal of the firm of Chat and Klein, an occupation which gave him "the means to afford the luxury of writing."[4] His interests have not been confined to legal work and poetry. He made an unsuccessful attempt to enter politics as a C.C.F. (Socialist) candidate, was for a time editor of the *Canadian Jewish Chronicle,* and taught for several years after the war as a guest lecturer in modern poetry at McGill.

Klein is one of the most autobiographical of Canadian poets, yet the poetry contained in the collected volumes does not give an accurate picture of his development as a poet. He has published five works: *Hath Not A Jew,* 1940; *Poems,* 1944; *The Hitleriad,* 1944; *The Rocking Chair and Other Poems,* 1948; and *The Second Scroll,* an allegorical novel, 1951.

The dates of publication are deceptive. The poems collected in *Hath Not a Jew,* published in 1940, had nearly all been written in the late Twenties and early Thirties. The long poem, "Greeting on this Day," seemed particularly appropriate for Jewry in 1940:

> Lest grief clean out the sockets of your eyes,
> Lest anguish purge your heart of happiness,
> Lest you go shaking fists at passive skies,
> And mouthing blasphemies in your distress,
> Be silent. Sorrow is a leper; shun
> The presence of his frosted phantom. Plant
> Small stones for eyes so that no tears may run,
> And underneath your ribs set adamant.

Yet this poem was written in 1929, in Klein's twentieth year, after riots in Palestine. Most of the other poems in this volume were written before 1934, many of them being mentioned by Collin in *The White Savannahs,* 1936.

For convenieince I divide Klein's work into five clearly marked periods of poetic development, for while early critical assessments often overlooked the uncollected

---

[4]*Saturday Night,* LXV (23 May 1950), 12.

poetry, and suggested that Klein's early intense orientation towards exclusively Jewish themes developed directly into French-Canadian subjects, this is only partly true. It is illuminating to examine the first four stages of Klein's development in terms of the fifth, represented by *The Second Scroll*—a work which unifies and imposes a clear pattern upon the other four.

The Second Scroll is an allegorical novel which presents the spiritual odyssey of the intellectual Jew in the contemporary world. The five chapters are Genesis, Exodus, Leviticus, Numbers and Deuteronomy—the five books of the Pentateuch, the First Scroll or Torah.

The narrator tells in the first chapter, Genesis, of his childhood and early manhood; how, from his earliest days, he heard of the Law of Moses, of the Talmud and the Torah, and of his fabulous Uncle Melech (King) far away, revered in Jewry as one of the truly great sages and interpreters of the Scriptures. The boy wants to become, like his uncle, a learned rabbi. But a terrible blow falls. Uncle Melech, living in Poland, has become bitter; his faith totters, and in the boy's home his name is mentioned no more. The Fall of Man is repeated in the new Genesis. An examination of Klein's early poetry, up to 1932, shows evidence of this first stage of development, the stage Klein describes in "Autobiographical," the first of the five Glosses in *The Second Scroll*:

> Out of the ghetto streets where a Jewboy
> Dreamed pavement into pleasant Bible-land,
> Out of the Yiddish slums where childhood met
> The friendly beard, the loutish Sabbath-goy,
> Or followed, proud, the Torah-escorting band,
> Out of the jargoning city I regret,
> Rise memories, like sparrows rising from
> The gutter-scattered oats,
> Like sadness sweet of synagogal hum,
> Like Hebrew violins
> Sobbing delight upon their Eastern notes.

The early poems share this exotic tone. After giving up his desire to be a rabbi, Klein turned his extensive knowledge of Jewish history and religion to the composition of a distinctive poetry. The forms and references are bewildering in their range. One may catch fleeting echoes from Chaucer, Shakespeare, Keats, Byron, Eliot and nursery rhymes, all pressed into the service of a Hebriac theme.

But there are those who are not true to their traditions, the false prophets who must be cast off, as Uncle Melech was:

> He quotes the Commentaries, yea,
> To Tau from Aleph,—
> But none the less, his tenants pay,
> Or meet the bailiff.
>   ("Landlord")

In the fifth Semitic Sonnet, written in 1930, Klein satirizes those Jews who would try to renounce their "noble lineage —proud ancestry" for expediency's sake:

> Now will we suffer loss of memory;
> We will forget the tongue our mothers knew;
> We will munch ham, and guzzle milk thereto,
> And this on hallowed feast-days, purposely . . .
> Abe will elude his base nativity.
> The kike will be a phantom; we will rue
> Our bearded ancestry, my nasal cue,
> And like the Gentiles we will strive to be.
> Our recompense: emancipation day.
> We will have friends where once we had a foe.
> Impugning epithets will glance astray.
> To gentile parties we will proudly go;
> And Christians, anecdoting us, will say:
> "Mr. and Mrs. Klein—the Jews, you know . . ."

Klein's bitterness is not against the Gentiles, but against the self-betrayal which is involved. A man is his traditions and his values; he cannot renounce them without destroying himself and shaming those he has left. But Klein can be less astringent. He pokes fun gently at old Reb.

Abraham who

> . . . loved Torah
> If followed by a feast,
> a milah-banquet, or a
> Schnapps to drink at least

Of Klein's early sequence of twenty-four sonnets written between 1928 and 1932, only five are reprinted in *Hath Not a Jew* under the heading of "Sonnets Semitic." While the omission strengthens the unity of the volume, the other sonnets reveal interesting side-lights to Klein's development as a poet. There are five experimental troubadour sonnets, of which only one, the first, is reprinted in *Hath Not a Jew*. There are six love sonnets, which Collin pessimistically considered the finest love poems in Canadian literature.

In a review of *Hath Not a Jew*, Louis Dudek commented:

> *Hath Not a Jew* is religious poetry, illuminated by the shining image of Klein's father, the father-image of Hamlet's piercing cry: "My father in his habit as he lived." The religious emotions, therefore, are not a response to the demands of a whole personality, but the idealism of a growing mind, a romantic expression of boyhood loves.

This judgement is only partly true, and one feels that Dudek would have altered it had he written after the publication of *The Second Scroll*. It is clear from this work that the religious emotions were the response to the demands of the whole personality, interpreted in this first period by idealism and romanticism. The Fifth Sonnet

(reprinted as Sonnet I in *Hath Not a Jew*) provides the
clearest example of Klein's romanticism at this stage:

> Would that three centuries past had seen us born!
> When gallants brought a continent on a chart
> To turreted ladies waiting their return.
> Then had my gifts in truth declared my heart!
> From foreign coasts, over tempestuous seas,
> I would have brought a gold-caged parakeet;
> Gems from some painted tribe; the Sultan's keys;
> Bright coronets; and placed them at your feet.
> Yea, on the high seas raised a sombre flag,
> And singed unwelcome beards, and made for shore
> With precious stones, and coins in many a bag
> To proffer you. These deeds accomplished, or
> I would have been a humble thin-voiced Jew
> Hawking old clo'es in ghetto lanes, for you.

However, as Uncle Melech changed, so did Klein. By
1932 Genesis was over and Exodus was about to begin. In
The Second Scroll (pp. 24-25) the narrator is about to
visit the newly-created state of Israel, when he hears of his
uncle and feels impelled to search for him. The rest of
the book is taken up with this search. As the Biblical Book
of the Exodus is divided into three parts: the enslavement,
the redemption and the setting apart of Israel, so too the
search is divided. We learn at last the cause of Melech's
disgrace:

Uncle Melech had joined the Bolsheviks! To my father
this was tantamount to apostasy. . . . My father was no
pharisee who stood shocked at a man's changing of his
political convictions. . . . Nor was my father a man to be
startled by rebellion; he himself had rebelled against the
Romanovs—through flight. But Bolshevism—
    Bolshevism meant the denial of the Name. . . . My
mother would try to defend her brother's action—what he
had lived through, she said, had upset his judgement—God
spare us all such a testing. But it was an unconvinced

defence and one that knew, even while it was being made, the arguments of its rebuttal. For it was clear that other people, too, had witnessed the pogrom and yet had not turned from their faith; many, moreover, had perished while Uncle Melech had been saved; and even of the perished—what was man, to question the will of God?

Thus does Klein, almost twenty years later, write of himself.

His second stage as a poet began in 1932. "The Ballad of Signs and Wonders" marked the beginning of a period of social protest poetry that was to punctuate the next seven years. The influence of T. S. Eliot is followed in rapid succession by that of Auden, Day Lewis and Spender. The poems are poor, a judgement confirmed by their omission from any of the volumes of collected poems. Some show an Elizabethan-Hebrew combination of epithet and invective, others a cynical world-weariness, and the themes range from the injustice of capitalism to the loss of his own faith through inability to believe in the co-existence of human suffering and divine justice.[5] It was common enough in the Thirties, but with Klein, the violence of the repudiation of those absolutes on which he had hitherto based his life was to have a lasting effect: the principles were to remain, hidden but intact, until he was to apply them in a context far wider than that which had given them birth. With the outbreak of the second world war the search for solutions turned inward, and Klein shared, on a personal level, the horror which had given to the "setting apart of Israel" a new and terrible inversion. The biblical Leviticus contains a restatement of the

[5]Most of the long poems of this period were published in *Canadian Forum*, with many shorter ones in *Poetry, Jewish Standard* and *New Names*. The successive influence of Eliot, Auden, Day Lewis and Spender may be seen most clearly in such poems as "The Diary of Abraham Segal, Poet" (May 1932), "The Soirée of Velvel Kleinburger" (August 1932), "Blueprint for a Monument of War" (September 1937), "Of Castles in Spain" (June 1938), "Barricade Smith" (November 1938).

Mosaic Law in order to unite the people of Israel. So Klein began his third period, which lasted from 1939 to 1942, by crying with Jeremiah: "Wherefore doth the way of the wicked prosper?" entreating the Lord to restore in him the faith he once had:

> These, then, the soothsayers, and this their reason:
> But where, O where is that inspired peasant,
> That prophet not of the remote occasion,
> But who will explicate the folded present?[6]

The spiritual drought is emphasized even more strongly in "A Psalm of Abraham, when he hearkened to a voice, and there was none."

The 1944 volume, *Poems*, is made up largely of verses composed during this third period, although some were written in the early Thirties. Klein has imposed a type of order upon these poems, and has divided them into three parts. The first group consists of psalms seeking the grace of the Lord for his people; the second is a series of anti-Nazi poems; the third, akin in some ways to the final sections of Eliot's "Ash Wednesday," is a description of a pilgrimage towards faith. As in Leviticus, the Law is still there to be restated in the individual heart—there are no prophets, each man must be his own explicator; if there is any hope this is where it must lie:

> Liveth the tale, nor ever shall it die!
> The princess in her tower grows not old.
> For that she heard his charmed minstrelsy,
> She is forever young. Her crown of gold,
> Bartered and customed, auctioned, hawked and sold,
> Is still for no head but her lovely head.
> What if the couch be hard, the cell be cold,
> The warder's keys unrusted, stale the bread?
> Halevi sang her song, and she is comforted.

---

[6]*Poems*, 1944, Jewish Publication Society, Philadelphia (1944), 31.

But it is a comfort that contains no forgiveness of the oppressors of Jewry. If each man is to be his own prophet let him also be given the power of vengeance to hurl the wicked from their heights:

> Grant me Thy grace, thy mortal touch,
> The full death-quiver of Thy wrath.

This is a theme continued in *The Hitleriad,* also published in 1944 (by New Directions, New York)—a stream of anti-Nazi invective which adds little to Klein's poetic stature, and says nothing not already said (with much greater insight) in *Poems.*

Klein's fourth period, 1942 to 1948, corresponds to the Book of Numbers, an account of the wanderings of the Jews among foreign peoples and in foreign lands. Before 1942 Klein regarded himself as one of these isolated and homeless members of his tribe, but after this date his outlook, hitherto restricted to his own people, broadened and began its exploratory wanderings.

It is in the poetry of this fourth period, represented by *The Rocking Chair and Other Poems,* that the process of synthesis begins to find expression. On the one hand is the historical tradition of Zion, of persecution, and of hope in impending liberation, in which the eternal minority will, after two thousand years, become a majority in its own national state. On the other hand is Klein's personal Canadian experience of minority-majority relations in his own city and homeland.

Klein's early comprehension of Jewry was a process of self-definition. It gave him roots, the answers to his questions, a sense of belonging, even a sense of cohesion caused by the discrimination against his race practised by some of those outside it. This sense of "Jewishness"—of belonging—provides a ready-made rampart from which to view those outside. Though the process of definition operates like this in most of the world, in Canada it must be modi-

fied, and for Klein the establishment of Israel, the concrete, public embodiment of this need for the minority to
feel that it is a majority *somewhere,* was not only a source
of satisfaction but of liberation.

In his fourth period Klein looks again, with new eyes,
on the environment so familiar to him but which he had
never really seen before. *The Rocking Chair* volume contains no poems which are specifically Jewish. He looks at
his French-Canadian compatriots, at the familiar artifacts
of the culture and the landscape, and experiences a shock
of recognition. The familiar rocking chair of the *habitant,*
which gives its title to the collection, becomes the symbol
of his discovery of a whole people:

> It rolls with the gait of St. Malo. It is act
>
> and symbol, symbol of this static folk
> which moves in segments, and returns to base—
> a sunken pendulum: invoke, revoke;
> loosed yon, leashed hither, motion on no space.
> O, like some Anjou ballad, all refrain,
> which turns about its longing and seems to move
> to make a pleasure out of repeated pain,
> its music moves, as if always back to a first love.

These surely are instincts which Klein recognizes and
understands: emphasis on the unity of the family, tradition, religion, rites and ceremonies, dogged perseverance
with a cultural inheritance maintained among those with
other traditions and other values—in other words the experience of a minority. All these Klein had known too,
and suddenly these people are not alien after all. He is
almost one with them, but not quite, for there are other
discoveries to be made.

As the French Canadians (a majority in Quebec) had
turned out to be a minority after all, what of the country
outside: the English-speaking majority? He tells of his
discovery in a poem called "The Provinces." They too
resist categorization. Each province has its own personality;

none wishes to be lumped in with the others. There is no "majority," in the orthodox sense, there. Then what keeps them together? What does "Canada" mean? He tries to suggest an answer, and it is the one which emerges from his own background and experience:

> But the heart seeks one, the heart, and also the mind
> seeks single the thing that makes them one, if one.
>   Yet where shall one find it? In their history—
> the cairn of cannonball on the public square?
> Their talk, their jealous double-talk? Or in
> the whim and weather of a geography
> curling in drifts about the forty-ninth?
> Or find it in the repute of character:
> romantic as mounties? Or discover it
> in beliefs that say:
> this is a country of Christmas trees?
>   Or hear it sing
> from the house with towers, from whose towers ring
> bells, and the carillon of laws?
> Where shall one find it? What
> to name it, that is sought?
> The ladder that nine brothers hold by the rungs?
> The birds that shine on each other? The white water
> that foams from the ivy entering their eaves?
>
> Or find it, find it, find it commonplace
> but effective, valid, real, the unity
> in the family feature, the not unsimilar face?

This tentative conclusion might seem unsatisfactory to a non-Canadian, but Klein's discovery of the "not unsimilar face" is, at the core, a very positive statement indeed. The very indirectness of the double negative avoids the suggestion of a common mould into which all must fit. From the basis of Jewry, Klein has emerged with an insight which has enabled him to give one of the most satisfying answers to the question of Canadian identity. But if there is no real majority is there really a minority either? Variations on this theme are examined in other poems in *The Rocking Chair*.

"Grain Elevator" admirably shows how Klein is able to endow the most mundane and familiar aspects of his Canadian environment with a complex tapestry of images and meanings. In the process, the uncompromising angles of the cement bulk of the elevator incorporate as a montage (not an overlay) the successive associations which are heaped upon it. The result is its metamorphosis to an absolute—the traditional absolute of bread—the flour which "flowers over us" as a symbol of common need. But the final image is not one that absorbs all the others within itself in a neat unity. The multiplicity remains:

Up from the low-roofed dockyard warehouses
it rises blind and babylonian
like something out of legend. Something seen
in a children's coloured book. Leviathan
swamped on our shore? The cliffs of some other river?
The blind ark lost and petrified? A cave
built to look innocent, by pirates? Or
some eastern tomb a travelled patron here makes local?

But even when known, it's more than what it is:
for here, as in a Josephdream, bow down
the sheaves, the grains, the scruples of the sun
garnered for darkness; and Saskatchewan
is rolled like a rug of a thick and golden thread.
O prison of prairies, ship in whose galleys roll
sunshines like so many shaven heads,
waiting the bushel-burst out of the beached bastille!

Sometimes, it makes me think Arabian,
the grain picked up, like tic-tacs out of time:
first one; an other; singly; one by one—
to save life. Sometimes, some other races claim
the twinship of my thought—as the river stirs
restless in a white Caucasian sleep,
or, as in the steerage of the elevators,
the grains, Mongolian and crowded, dream.

A box: cement, hugeness, and rightangles—
merely the sight of it leaning in my eyes
mixes up continents and makes a montage
of inconsequent time and uncontinguous space.
It's because it's bread. It's because
bread is its theme, an absolute. Because
always this great box flowers over us
with all the coloured faces of mankind. . . .

There is still a residual note of loss sometimes sounded.
In "The Cripples," describing the pilgrims to the shrine
at St Joseph's Oratory in Montreal, Klein concludes:

And I who in my own faith once had faith like this
but have not now, am crippled more than they.

But the components of Klein's new and more encompass-
ing faith are already being assembled. There are, inevitably, some dead ends in his explorations. Besides his
interest in Hopkins and James Joyce, some of the poems
experiment with the linguistic problems of Canadian
poetry. In an introduction to "Parade of St Jean Baptiste,"
not included in *The Rocking Chair,* Klein describes his
intentions:

This is one of a series of experimental poems, making
trial of what I flatter myself to believe is a "bilingual
language," since the vocabulary of the poem is mainly of
Norman and Latin origin. There is no word in it (with
the exception of articles and auxiliary words) which has
not a relationship or similarity to a synonymous word in
the French language.[7]

"Montreal," in *The Rocking Chair,* is an example of this
technique:

Grand port of navigations, multiple
The lexicons uncargo'd at your quays,
Sonnant though strange to me; but chiefest, I,

---

[7]*Canadian Forum*, XXVII, 258-9.

> Auditor of your music, cherish the
> Joined double-melodied vocabulaire
> Where English vocable and roll Ecossic,
> Mollified by the parle of French
> Bilinguefact your air!

It is interesting that Klein should have carried his search for synthesis so far, but this is too close to the idea of the melting pot, and it will not do in Canada. Understandably, French Canadians took a greater interest in *The Rocking Chair* than in most collections of poems published in English. One reviewer observed:

La source de cette fantasie se trouve une âme qui vibre à l'unisson de la nôtre, soit devant la piété émouvante des pèlerins de l'Oratoire, la pédanterie choquante de M. Bertrand ou la coquetterie des villages laurentiens.

And, on Klein's place as a poet:

L'expression est en anglais, mais les sujets et les évocations sont tellement nôtres que l'auteur ne pouvait plus clairement dire combien il a vibré aux charmes naturels et spirituels de notre patrie.[8]

It is in the book's longest poem, "Portrait of the Poet as Landscape," that Klein's exploration of the isolation of the individual is combined with the theme of the inevitable isolation of the artist, forced by his creative imagination to

> . . . [seed] illusions. Look, he is
> the nth Adam taking a green inventory
> in world but scarcely uttered, naming, praising,
> the flowering fiats in the meadow, the
> syllable fur, stars aspirate, the pollen
> whose sweet collision sounds eternally.
> For to praise
> the world—he, solitary man—is breath

---

[8]*Relations*, June 1948, 184-5.

to him. Until it has been praised, that part
has not been. Item by exciting item—
air to his lungs, and pressured blood to his heart—
they are pulsated, and breathed, until they map,
not the world's, but his own body's chart!

As the creative act applied to the external world is also an
act of self-creation, in the sense of self-discovery, it is
necessarily solitary; and meanwhile the poet

makes of his status as zero a rich garland
a halo of his anonymity,
and lives alone, and in his secret shines
like phosphorus. At the bottom of the sea.

If this fourth phase may be likened to the wanderings of
the Book of Numbers, the fifth, which has lasted from
1948 to the present, has all the character of Deuteronomy.
There is a repetition of the Law, for those who have come
to forget, a summary and synthesis of first principles
repeated on the approaching entrance of the Israelites to
their Promised Land. With the publication of *The Second
Scroll* in 1951 the pattern of Klein's poetry may be seen
whole.

The narrator, the poet, is still seeking his Uncle Melech,
a projection of Klein's spiritual self. There is what one
might call a trichotomy of parallels throughout: the
ancient tribulations of the Jewish people, their modern
re-enactment, the spiritual Odyssey of Klein himself.

Genesis, the first stage, is based on a firm conviction of
faith—an almost lyrical acceptance of the verse:

And I will bless them that bless thee, and curse him that
curseth thee; and in thee shall all families of the earth be
blessed.[9]

But as Man fell and lost the Garden of Eden, and as
modern Jewry showed signs of turning away from God, so

[9]Genesis xii, 3.

too did Klein turn to materialism during the Depression.
The State of Man (and Klein) before the Fall is represented in the volume *Hath Not a Jew*.

The second, Exodus, progressed as Melech turned from
religious faith to Communism, seeking in it the answers
which he believed he had sought in vain from God. In the
black days of the depression Klein too turned from faith.
This period is represented by the uncollected poetry of
social protest. Neither Klein, nor his spiritual self, Melech,
had sufficient faith to follow Moses across the wilderness:

And Moses said: this shall be, when the Lord shall give you
in the evening flesh to eat, and in the morning bread to
the full; for that the Lord heareth your murmurings which
ye murmur against him: and what are we? your murmurings are not against us but again the Lord.[10]

In the third, Leviticus, God has laid down his commandments for the children of Israel:

If ye walk in my statutes, and keep my commandments,
and do them . . . I will walk among you, and will be your
God, and ye shall be my people. . . . But if ye will not
hearken unto me, and will not do all those commandments
. . . I will set my face against you, and ye shall be slain
before your enemies: they that hate you shall reign over
you. . . .[11]

Neither Klein nor his race had observed the Covenant.
This is the period of the Psalms and *The Hitleriad*—the
people of Israel are again in anguish, and Melech, as
Klein's projection, endures the agonies of a German prison
camp.

The fourth section, Numbers, tells how, after the de-
liverance in 1945, the narrator went to Italy in search of
this uncle whom he had never seen. He had intended to
go straight to Israel, but was deflected on the way. He

[10]Exodus xvi, 8.
[11]Leviticus xxvi, 3, 12, 14, 17.

found that Melech had gone to Rome, had talked with the
Catholic clergy, and had gone to the Sistine Chapel to
study Christian art. From a letter he discovers Melech's
reactions. He had come to the conclusion that since Adam
was created in the image of God, the killing of man is
deicide, and that as Eve is a reproductive creature, the
murder of the mortal is a murder of the immortal. Here
there is a deviation from the Old Testament. There, the
Lord called for a census of all the chosen—the people of
Israel. Here, Klein is embracing all humanity in a common
brotherhood as the sons of God. But he was not yet ready
to commit himself fully; study of Catholicism was only a
flirtation.

The Rocking Chair was not a final statement; it was
part of the search for self-identification, a questioning
which must probe and analyse all parts of the poet's
environment. It is true that Klein has always belonged to
the minority: Jewry, Socialism, French Canada, but
through these he has come to see that there need be no
minority. The solution could not be approached earlier
because there was still an infatuation with suffering; but
now the ecumenical statement may be made, and it rings
out at the conclusion of the fourth Gloss in *The Second
Scroll*:

Jew: What is it stands between us? Not disbelief!
　　　We worship all the same great sovereign Lord;
　　　In gesture and in genuflection differ,
　　　Differ only in choice of him we send
　　　With our soul's embassy to the throne of God;
　　　In all other respects we do not differ.
　　　For hear, O Cadi, there is but one God!
　　　His is the light, the one transcendent light
　　　Illuminating the dome of heaven and
　　　The little alcoves of the private heart.
　　　His prophets and vicars, porters of His flame
　　　Announce the light—but their's is not the light.
　　　The light is God's! That light sees all.

The final stage is reached. Melech does go to Israel and there almost at once dies a martyr's death in a skirmish with Arab raiders. He is burnt to death with gasoline, and his features are unrecognizable; appropriately, in death, he becomes the symbol—the pillar of fire—of modern Israeli determination to preserve the new-found redemption. But through Melech's martyrdom the narrator has finished his pilgrimage and is at peace. He can return to Canada with the knowledge that his people have assumed their inheritance. There is no longer a need for the masochism of minority self-assertion. The Law is not a sectional shibboleth, it is only one way of stating the universal truth. He can thus return to Jewry not as a defence against those who think differently, but as one who has his place in the mosaic, adding richness to the design. The First Scroll of the Old Testament had not been read to reach such all-embracing conclusions, yet in essence it is the same. All that love God, no matter what their creed, are the new children of Israel, and that is why this is the *Second* Scroll. The book ends:

> Thou hast turned for me my mourning into dancing
> thou has put my sackcloth and girded me
> with gladness.
>   To the end that my glory may sing praise to thee,
> and not be silent, O Lord my God,
> I will give thanks unto thee for ever.

As Joyce composed a new odyssey for the Dubliner, Klein has written a second scroll for modern Jewry. The period of the Pentateuch is over, and Klein has responded to the challenge "to sing unto the Lord a new song."

Theorems Made Flesh:
Klein's Poetic Universe

[handwritten annotation: this article pts to his similarities with white traditionalists both, in themes + images]

Tom Marshall

This article appeared in Canadian Literature *No. 25.*

Tom Marshall began his study of Klein in 1964 in an M.A. thesis for Queen's University. He is the author of one book of poems, The Silences of Fire *(Macmillan, 1969) and of* The Psychic Mariner *(The Viking Press, 1970), a study of the poems of D. H. Lawrence.*

> O, he who unrolled our culture from his scroll . . .
>
> and a third, alone, and sick with sex, and rapt,
> doodles him symbols convex and concave. . . .
>
> ("Portrait of the Poet as Landscape")

At first I saw only geometry: triangle consorting with square, circle rolling in rectangle, the caress parabolic, the osculations of symmetry: as if out of old time Euclid were come to repeat his theorems now entirely in terms of anatomy. Theorems they are, but theorems made flesh. . . .

(Gloss Gimel, *The Second Scroll*)

From the above examples, which could easily be multiplied, one can see that the world of Abraham Klein is very often seen in terms of a book (or scroll) or as a system of geometry. For he believes with the Spinoza of his "Out of the Pulver and the Polished Lens" that the order in the universe can be grasped by the intellect. One can reduce

providence to theorems and set these down in a book; the
book or system of order devised by man (including, of
course, any work of art) is a metaphor for total reality.

There are good reasons for this in Klein's cultural heritage. Jews do not, like Roman Catholics, venerate images,
but they do venerate the holy scroll itself in its physical
aspect. This consists of sheets of parchment sewn together
into a scroll rolled at each end onto a piece of wood. In a
scroll the Hebrew is copied out letter by letter by hand,
and the words must remain exactly as they have been for
over two thousand years. The very letters must be preserved, and are venerated as sacred objects.

Hebrew letters are very versatile. They can be used to
render numbers (e.g. Yod-Aleph for 11), and the pages of
the Talmud are numbered in this way. The letter Hai is
especially significant since it is used as a short form of the
tetragrammaton or four-letter abbreviation of the name of
God. Klein concludes *The Second Scroll* with his Gloss
Hai, a liturgy affirming the ultimate goodness of God's
design.

For Hebrew cabbalists letters and numbers have special
hidden significances. It seems certain that Klein, who begins a poem "I am no contradictor of Cabbala. . . ," has
been influenced by this sort of mysticism.[1] The idea of
Jerusalem as princess (employed in "Yehuda Halevi, His
Pilgrimage") and the interpretation of the Song of Songs
in terms of spiritual marriage are Cabbalistic. Safed, a city
Klein celebrates in "Greeting on this Day" and *The Second
Scroll*, is chiefly noted for the school of Cabbalistic mystics
who flourished there after the expulsion of the Jews from
Spain.

The Cabbala divides itself into the speculative Cabbala,
which is the "contemplation of the sensual world as it
sprang from the spiritual essence of the Deity," and the
practical Cabbala, which is "the Talismanic use of divine

[1]A. M. Klein, "Desideratum," *Contemporary Verse* (June-Sept. 1943), 3.

names and words for the accomplishment of certain ends."
The ultimate goal is the kingdom of the Messiah.[2]

Klein exhibits a concern for "practical" cabbala in
"Talisman in Seven Shreds." This sonnet sequence employs the legend of the golem or robot created by the rabbi
to aid persecuted Jewry. In the legend the golem is brought
to life by the placement under his tongue of a piece of
parchment bearing the tetragrammaton, but the speaker of
Klein's poem mourns the loss of the magic formula.

By way of contrast, we might note that Isaac Luria (1533-
72), the chief cabbalist of Safed, "invented a whole system
of amulets, conjurations, mystic jugglery with words and
numbers, and a process of ascetic practices whereby the
powers of evil might be overcome."[3]

The Cabbala was very influential in Poland, the land of
Klein's ancestors, after the sixteenth century. Here was
founded Chassidism, a mystical reform movement which
aimed at a more direct experience of the divine soul, and
here abounded individuals "who, by manipulating the letters spelling out the Divine Name, were believed to exercise authority over Spirits."[4] Klein customarily speaks of
illness in terms of possession by defiant evil spirits, and
notes the benevolent presence within himself of his ancestors in "Psalm XXXVI, a psalm touching genealogy."

The Cabbala "taught a doctrine of unbroken intercourse
between God and the world." God's creation is matter, but
is "ablaze with soul." God needs to establish His identity:

He is the *En Sof,* the Endless or Boundless one, who, like
Spinoza's substance, cannot be designated by any known
attribute, but who is best called *Ayin* (Non-existent).
Hence in order to make His existence known at all, the
Deity was obliged or wished to reveal Himself to at least
some extent. In other words, He had to become active and
creative in order to make Himself manifest.[5]

[2]"Cabbala," *Universal Jewish Encyclopedia,* Vol. II, 614-15.
[3]"Cabbala," *Universal Jewish Encyclopedia,* Vol. II, 618.
[4]Ibid.
[5]Ibid., 619.

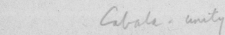

God here seems to be motivated by the same need that motivates Klein's poet in "Portrait of the Poet as Landscape." Creation is self-realization; one must create in order "to be." The poet's attempt at self-definition through art parallels God's desire to make himself manifest. More than this, it is an attempt to realize the godhead innate in every man and is thus an approach to the Messianic kingdom of the spirit.

The Cabbala has supported its more extreme doctrines by giving the letters, words and names of the Bible special meanings. This can be done by using the numerical equivalents of the letters, by treating individual letters as initials or abbreviations of other words, or by substituting the preceding or following letter of the alphabet. Klein does not indulge in such extreme verbal jugglery, but his attempts at a bilingual poetry and the significance he attaches to alphabetical characters (and to puns and other figures of speech), can be considered in the light of the Cabbalistic belief in the magic properties of language. Klein may not share the literal belief in magic, but he is certainly influenced by it.

Thus, when he discusses the faith of French-Canadians, it is natural for him to see a wall-crucifix as an "agonized Y". Similarly, it is natural for him to think of art as a divine faculty. Michelangelo is for Klein in much more than a trivial sense the Archangel Michael. For the world is One, and art is a kind of communication with the perfect whole. Man collaborates in God's continuous creation. Therefore a connection in language (and, by extension, any connection of any system — whether it be geometry, heraldry or the law) is a true statement about the whole universe. Seeing creation whole is a matter of partaking in it through the activity of metaphor.

It is useful, after this introduction, to examine the development of those persistent and recurrent metaphors that give to Klein's particular vision of the universe the coherence of myth. We have seen how persistent in his work is the general notion of the universe as God's writ; we may now briefly consider the most important features of the microcosm that is Klein's writ.

The figure that dominates Klein's earliest poetry is certainly the Jew as dwarf or clown and, more important, as martyr and wanderer. The clown is an aspect of the martyr; hunted and persecuted by his enemies, the Jew defends himself by narrowing the scope of his world and by a retreat into self-deprecating humour. "I will dwarf myself," declares Childe Harold, "and live in a hut." This dwarfing process can be seen in the creation of the comic and charming fairy-tale world that takes up most of the latter part of *Hath Not A Jew*. Here is a pleasant diminutive world peopled by dwarfs, children, homunculi and elves. Love prevails, and life's problems are scaled down, as in "Bestiary," where a little Jewish boy is able to hunt down the persecuting beast, Nebuchadnezzar, in the pages of the Bible. This poetry is full of the association of the words "little" and "Jew." The little, it seems, can be enough if it is self-contained and self-sustaining, as in "Dr. Dwarf," where all ills are cured by the magic of the Doctor, a sort of diminutive Messiah.

But the Jew is also engaged in a more positive struggle, the journey back to Zion. This journey is for Klein a symbolic representation of each individual's struggle to achieve wholeness within himself and harmony with his environment. Israel is to be both a physical and a spiritual homecoming for the Jew; the miracle operates on a cultural and a personal level. The goal can be seen in terms of the young poet's love for a beloved woman. She is seen as the fair princess of chivalry, and the union with her is analogous to the spiritual marriage of God and his people on their Holy Land.

Because a "Christian" civilization has betrayed the ideals of chivalry in mistreating the Jews, Klein is able in "Childe Harold's Pilgrimage" to describe the swastika as "a cross with claws." But he borrows the conventions of mediaeval chivalry to express his vision of the quest for Zion that is also the quest for personal integrity.

Both personal love and Zionism are related to the cyclic pattern of nature. In the activities of love and procreation man exists in harmony with the purposes of nature. On the land Israel the Jewish people can exist as an organic unity in a way that it cannot in the ghetto of cultural solidarity. Nevertheless, this cultural unity is also related to the cycle of nature, though at one remove from it. For it is the symbolic expression of the soul of the people in past generations and it needs only to be reunited with the land to take on a new vitality.

Underlying Klein's use of the natural cycle is a concept of the eternal unchanging order of things. Klein believes in an ultimate order, in an absolute justice that will ensure Jewry's recovery. Thus he often employs the figure of the circle, the perfect expression of the world's unity, and speaks in "Out of the Pulver and the Polished Lens" of the One creation that is contained in God:

For thou art the world, and I am part thereof; he who does violence to me, verily sins against the light of day; he is made a deicide.[6]

Man is a part of the One, a fragment praying unto perfection.

As a circle that must periodically re-establish itself as a circle, the moon is a fit symbol for the fluctuating human power of creativity. Klein's moon focuses within itself all the welter of human emotions with which wholeness must be fashioned. The poet of "Business" is "a hawker of the moon," and Klein speaks in "Preface" of poetic fame as a matter of setting one's thumbprint on the moon. The moon is identified with an amazing variety of objects—

[6]The passage, "he who does violence . . . a deicide", which is strikingly similar to Melech's remarks about deicide in *The Second Scroll*, does not occur in *Hath Not A Jew* . . . but only in the poem's original publication in *The Canadian Forum*, XI (1931), 453-54.

charming or grand or sinister—in Klein's early poetry. It is usually an indicator of his mood and the focus of his poetic universe.

In "Greeting on this Day" terrified Jews "see the moon drip gore." In "Design for Mediaeval Tapestry" the moon is "a rude gargoyle in the sky" of a Christian and Judæo-phobic world. But in "Out of the Pulver and the Polished Lens" the moon is God's "little finger's fingernail," and in "Haggadah" it is a golden platter in the sky.

In "Letters to One Absent" the moon is a mirror in which lovers find each other, and in "Psalm XXI" it is the seal of God upon his open writ; it appears to be the creative lens for both God and man, that area of the soul in which man and God are joined. The force that enables man to love and to create works of art analogous to God's creation is the God within him. The moon may then be said to function in Klein's early poetry as a symbolic expression of the creative world-soul.

It is significant, then, that in the time of his greatest disillusionment and doubt about the nature of the order in the universe Klein's moon becomes a "smooth hydraulic dynamo." For the poetry of the middle and late thirties suggests that if there is a God man has no meaningful contact with him. The tetragrammaton, the talisman that once enabled man to exercise the creative power of the God within, has been shredded and has lost its efficacy.

The figure that dominates this poetry is the golem or mechanical man. In this perfectly mechanical and mate-rialistic age the poet, who represents creative man, has become obsolete. In "Barricade Smith: His Speeches," which contains the image of the hydraulic moon, the poet is caricatured as a fool wasting his energies on "stars archaic and obsolete dew."

In "Manuscript: Thirteenth Century" Klein's fair princess, once the symbolic expression of love's fulfillment, gives herself to a villain and is brought to ruin, and in "Barricade Smith: His Speeches" she is demoted to debutante. Barricade Smith, like a true knight, loves her "from afar," but she marries first "the tenth cousin of the Czar" and then a "closer relative of a deposed king," whom she eventually divorces and gives two million dollars as "a little tip."

The poetry of the early forties, however, expresses the recovery from this disillusionment in a reassertion of the figures that dominated the earliest poetry. The Jew as wanderer or spiritual seeker, the fair princess, the Utopian land of Israel, the moon-mirror and the natural cycle are all restored to their original significances.

There are changes and new features, however. The notion of a cosmic court of law by which Jewry's enemies are to be condemned is introduced in order to suggest the justice that must ultimately prevail in the universe. Related to this is the curious fact that the comic dwarf and the mindless golem (or automaton) seem now to be combined in Hitler, the arch-villain and chief disruptive influence in Klein's universe. What had seemed mechanical and inhuman is not, it appears, of any ultimate significance. Hitler is nothing more than a frustrated little man on the rampage, even though the restoration of harmony in Klein's universe is now dependent upon his destruction.

It is interesting that Klein now refuses to see the Jew as a comic dwarf. The Jew as martyr and seeker after perfection has eclipsed the Jew as clown, and the godlike Uncle Melech is lurking in the wings.

In the poem "Autobiographical" (1943), which seems to mark the midpoint of Klein's development, the poet's personal quest for the "fabled city" of innocence and security foreshadows the career of Uncle Melech, but the city sought by this particular wandering Jew is not the actual Jerusalem (or even Safed); it is the enchanted Montreal of his childhood. This realization leads us inevitably to the truth that any city can be a fabled city, that each man has a personal Zion of the imagination.

This notion, which was at least implicit in Klein's earlier poetry, now brings him to the exploration of the Canadian scene that dominates the poetry of the late forties. This study of Canada provides another opportunity to express his view of man's place in the universe. The belief in man's divine creativity, his ability to unite himself to other men and even to God through self-expression, underlies the experiments in a bilingual poetry. Language is a substantial magic that can unite men in sympathy.

In the poetry of the "Canadian" period the figure of the dwarf-clown is found again, but he is not now a villain or a specifically Jewish hero. He is Everyman. He is individual man as a minority of one—as martyr and clown and wanderer and hero combined. He is the beleaguered and yet comical French-Canadian of "Political Meeting," the Indian in his "grassy ghetto," the lone bather immersed in animal delight, the isolated poet, and, finally, the "nth Adam," who is not only the poet but every man with the creative power of God lying dormant in him.

Because Klein is feeling his way into the problems of a Christian society in his French-Canadian poems he now gives to Christian symbols a more positive significance than he once did. This is, of course, a necessary consequence of the belief that Montreal may be as much a fabled city as Safed. Man's hopes can be centred upon the Oratoire de St. Joseph as well as Safed, or, more practically, upon a grain elevator. Klein's discovery of his favourite middle-eastern landscape in the "Josephdream" of the grain elevator signifies his realization that Utopia might be anywhere, though it is probably in Israel for the Jew. This enables us to see the Utopian Israel of *The Second Scroll* as a symbolic expression of every man's imagined home.

In this poetry we lose sight of the beautiful princess. Love is presented as a memory, a remembered magic at the top of Mount Royal. The creative moon, too, has vanished (though it reappears in *The Second Scroll* which concludes with "new moons, festivals and set times"). But the figure of the circle remains very prominent. We find (in "Portrait of the Poet as Landscape") "the mirroring lenses forgotten on a brow," and the poet wearing his zero as an ambiguous garland; we find both the natural cycle and its cultural equivalent in the movement of the rocking chair and the Anjou ballad.

For the first time water becomes very important. Since the sea is a traditional symbol for birth and renewal, it is curious that Klein, who was always concerned with various kinds of resurrection, did not use it before.[7] In *The Rocking Chair* he does so in order to suggest both the neglected state of the submerged poet and the birth of a shining new world in his imagination. The poet's submersion can be (like the cultural ghetto of the Jew) a kind of protection. It offers the comfort every man may take from the exercise of his imagination, and provides a home in the private world of memories and hopes. Klein writes in "Lookout: Mount Royal" of

> the photographer's tripod and his sudden faces
> buoyed up by water on his magnet caught
> still smiling as if under water still . . .

The deep well of memories, instincts and creative impulses can become one with the creative lens; thus, water serves the function the moon served in the early poetry.

The suggestion is that man can express his personal experience of the universe in the work of art, a distinct and communicable microcosm. In *The Rocking Chair* Klein re-creates childhood memories; in "And in That Drowning Instant" he submerges himself once again in racial and cultural memories, but surfaces, so to speak, in the re-creation of the experience as poetry.

---

[7]Milton Wilson has called *Hath Not A Jew* . . . "the driest book in Canadian poetry" (*Canadian Literature* No. 6, 12) because it has virtually no water imagery. But in *The Rocking Chair*, as Wilson notes, water is related to man's submerged life in such poems as "Portrait of the Poet as Landscape," "The Break-Up," "Dress Manufacturer: Fisherman," "Lookout: Mount Royal" and "Lone Bather."

In the poetry of *The Rocking Chair* geometry tends to replace law as the system used to suggest the ultimate order of the universe. This is a subtler way of expressing faith in the stability and unity of creation since it is less dependent than law upon human notions of morality. The further suggestion of the use of the alphabet and of scroll imagery is that the universe may contain a message from God.

Man's organized perception can at least approximate God's creativity. In "Krieghoff: Calligrammes" the artist employs a magic language to communicate with God, to participate in His creation. By ordering the "blank whiteness" of his experience he enables himself and his world to be known.

This brings us back to the solitary man who is Everyman. In *The Second Scroll* we find a protagonist, Uncle Melech, who, as the successor to Childe Harold, Solomon Warshawer and Yehuda Halevi, is the wandering Jew, and, thus, Jewry itself. He is also Abraham Klein. And beyond this he is the creative man, and, thus, the Messiah. For the Messiah can finally be identified as the creative man who seeks and discovers God in himself.

Klein's chief heroes—Spinoza, Yehuda Halevi, Euclid, Michelangelo—have always been creative men reaching to God and attempting to establish His order. Man is the nth Adam, a solitary individual whose task is that of every individual before him—to perceive and express and thus re-create the universe in order to define it as a context for himself. The God within, the lens, must focus in itself the whole of the God without. All self-expression, whether it result in a system of geometry, the Anjou ballad, a rocking chair, a Hebrew brand-name or the Sistine Chapel, is a means to this end.

Klein's own interpretation of the Sistine paintings is an exercise of language as magic. The ceiling is seen as geometry and expressed in language that vividly re-creates its physical presence at the same time as it describes the glory and the dangerous limitation that is the human condition. Man is depicted by Michelangelo ("say rather the Archangel Michael") as a potential god caught in the perilous wheels that seem to determine suffering and death. He is able to achieve divinity in an art that may communicate its infinite meaning to individuals of succeeding generations. Klein contends:

It well may be that Michelangelo had other paradigms in mind: there is much talk of Zimzum and retraction; but such is the nature of art that though the artist entertain fixedly but one intention and one meaning, that creation once accomplished beneath his hand, now no longer merely his own attribute, but Inspiration's very substance and entity, proliferates with significances by him not conceived or imagined. Such art is eternal and to every generation speaks with fresh coeval timeliness. In vain did Buonarotti seek to confine himself to the hermeneutics of his age; the Spirit intruded and lo! on that ceiling appeared the narrative of things to come, which came indeed, and behold above me the parable of my days.

Melech-Klein finds in the ceiling a prophecy both of the Jewish suffering of the twentieth century and of the Messianic era that is to follow. Here we certainly have art as a communication with God.

Klein's own art in Gloss Gimel involves the creation of a rich prose heightened by effects of sound, rhythm, sensual imagery and metaphor to the power of poetry, a language like that he employed in parts of "Out of the Pulver and the Polished Lens." With "Portrait of the Poet as Landscape," these are surely his most powerful and moving performances. Few English poets of the twentieth century have been capable of such sustained and concentrated and controlled passion. But then, few modern poets have retained the kind of belief in man and God that would enable them to see their own utterance as fiat.

BIBLIOGRAPHY

Books

Abraham Moses Klein. *Hath Not A Jew*. Foreword by Ludwig Lewisohn. New York: Behrman House Inc., 1940.

——. *The Hitleriad*. New York: New Directions, 1944.

——. *Poems 1944*. Philadelphia: Jewish Publication Society, 1944.

——. *The Rocking Chair*. Toronto: The Ryerson Press, 1948.

——. *The Second Scroll*. New York: Alfred A. Knopf, 1951.

Magazines

American Caravan

A. M. Klein. "Design for Mediaeval Tapestry," IV (1931), 351-57.

Canadian Forum

A. M. Klein. "Business," IX (1929), 379.

——. "Out of the Pulver and the Polished Lens," XI (1931), 453-54.

——. "Calvary," XII (1931), 58.

——. "Old Maid's Wedding," XII (1931), 58.

——. "Earthquake," XII (1932), 173.

——. "Philosopher's Stone," XII (1932), 173.

——. "Diary of Abraham Segal, Poet," XII (1932), 297-300.

——. "Soirée of Velvel Kleinburger," XII (1932), 424-25.

——. "Desiderata," XII (1932), 459.

——. "Wood Notes Wild," XIII (1932), 60.

——. "Anguish," XIII (1933), 257.

——. "Divine Titillation," XIII (1933), 331.

——. "Manuscript: Thirteenth Century," XIV (1934), 474-76.

——. "Beggars I Have Known," XVI (1936), 19-20.

——. "Blueprint for a Monument of War," XVII (1937), 208-209.

——. "Of Castles in Spain," XVIII (1938), 79.

——. "Barricade Smith: His Speeches," XVIII (1938), 147-48, 173, 210, 242-43.

——. "Ballad of the Thwarted Axe," XXI (1941), 212.

——. "Ballad of the Nursery Rhymes," XXI (1941), 244.

——. "Actuarial Report," XXIII (1943), 60.

——. "Autobiography," XXIII (1943), 106.

——. "That Legendary Eagle, Death," XXIII (1943), 127.

——. "Basic English," XXIV (1944), 138.

——. "Political Meeting," XXVI (1946), 136.

——. "Doctor Drummond," XXVI (1946), 136.

——. "The White Old Lady," XXVI (1946), 136.

——. "Parade of St. Jean Baptiste," XXVII (1948), 258-59.

Canadian Jewish Chronicle

A. M. Klein. "Ballad of Signs and Wonders," XV (1928), 9.

Canadian Mercury

A. M. Klein. "Haunted House," I (1929), 35.
———. "Fixity," I (1929), 110.

Canadian Poetry

A. M. Klein. "Quebec Liquor Commission," X (1946), 19-20.
———. "The Spinning Wheel," X (1946), 20-21.

Contemporary Verse

A. M. Klein. "Desideratum," Summer 1943, 3.
———. "Dress Manufacturer: Fisherman," Fall 1947, 3.
———. "O God! O Montreal," Fall 1947, 4.
———. "Monsieur Gaston," Fall 1947, 5.
———. "Meditation Upon Survival," Summer 1950, 9-10.

Dalhousie Review

A. M. Klein. "Seasons," XII (1932), 209.

First Statement

A. M. Klein. "The Hitleriad," II (1943), 1-3.
———. "A Psalm of Abraham, which he made because of fear in the night," II (1943), 1.
———. "A Psalm or Prayer—praying his portion with beasts," II (1943), 2.
———. "A Psalm of Abraham when he hearkened to a voice and there was none," II (1943), 2.
———. "Pawnshop," II (1945), 26-28.
———. "Portrait of the Poet as a Nobody," III (1945), 3-8.

Jewish Frontier

A. M. Klein. "A Psalm of Abraham on Madness," IX (1942), 8.

Menorah Journal

A. M. Klein. "Five Characters," XIII (1927), 497-98.
———. "Five Weapons Against Death," XV (1929), 49-51.
———. "Portraits of a Minyan," XVII (1929), 86-88.
———. "Greeting on this Day," XVIII (1930), 1-4.
———. "Talisman in Seven Shreds," XX (1932), 148-50.
———. "*In Re* Solomon Warshawer," XXVIII (1940), 138-40.
———. "Psalms of Abraham," XXIX (1941), 280-85.

Nation

A. M. Klein. "The Rocking Chair," CLXI (1945), 341.

Northern Review

A. M. Klein. "The Provinces," I (1945-46), 27-28.

Poetry

A. M. Klein. "A Sequence of Songs," XXXV (1929), 22-24.
———. "The Psalter of A. M. Klein," LVIII (1941), 6-8.
———. "Two Poems," LIX (1942), 315-17.
———. "Come Two, Like Shadows," LXI (1943), 595.
———. "Seven Poems," LXX (1947), 175-81.

Preview

A. M. Klein. "Variations on a Theme," July 1942, 9.
———. "Actuarial Report," March 1943, 7-8.
———. "Dentist," May 1944, 12.
———. "Montreal," Sept. 1944, 3-5.
———. "The Library," Dec. 1944, 10.
———. "The Green Old Age," Dec. 1944, 10-11.

Queen's Quarterly

A. M. Klein. "The Snowshoers," LIV (1947-48), 412.

Saturday Night

A. M. Klein. "Ballad of Quislings," LVI (Aug. 30, 1941), 25.
———. "Ballad of the Nuremburg Tower Clock," LVII (Nov. 8, 1941), 10.
———. "Polish Village," LVII (Jan. 31, 1942), 3.